GW00500110

Slow Cooker Recipe Book UK

1000 Days of Healthy, Affordable & Authentic British Dishes for Beginners & Advanced Users. Includes a 28-Days Healthy Meal Plan

By

Nathan Terrell

© Copyright 2023 by Nathan Terrell - All rights reserved.

This document is geared towards providing exact and reliable information in regards to the topic and issue covered. The publication is sold with the idea that the publisher is not required to render accounting, officially permitted, or otherwise, qualified services. If advice is necessary, legal or professional, a practiced individual in the profession should be ordered.

- From a Declaration of Principles, which was accepted and approved equally by a Committee of the American Bar Association and a Committee of Publishers and Associations.

In no way is it legal to reproduce, duplicate, or transmit any part of this document in either electronic means or in printed format. Recording of this publication is strictly prohibited, and any storage of this document is not allowed unless with written permission from the publisher. All rights reserved.

The information provided herein is stated to be truthful and consistent, in that any liability, in terms of inattention or otherwise, by any usage or abuse of any policies, processes, or directions contained within is the solitary and utter responsibility of the recipient reader. Under no circumstances will any legal responsibility or blame be held

against the publisher for any reparation, damages, or monetary loss due to the information herein, either directly or indirectly.

Respective authors own all copyrights not held by the publisher.

The information herein is offered for informational purposes solely and is universal as so. The presentation of the information is without contract or any type of guarantee assurance.

The trademarks that are used are without any consent, and the publication of the trademark is without permission or backing by the trademark owner. All trademarks and brands within this book are for clarifying purposes only and are owned by the owners themselves, not affiliated with this document.

Contents

Introduction

Traditional slow cooking will remain popular no matter how advanced the appliances and methods of modern kitchens become. The flavorful texture of many of the foods we eat is achieved only by slow, low cooking for long periods of time. For example, if you let beef or lamb simmer in its broth for several hours over low heat, the meat will develop a rich flavor. The same holds true for bean and lentil chili, as well as other vegetable soups. Because of the development of electric cookers, slow cooking is now much simpler, despite the fact that it takes time and can be challenging for some. Now you can put all your worries on the machine and sit back while it whips up delicious meals for you. The slow cooker will keep the food at the proper temperature for the specified amount of time.

Recipes for a wide range of foods from the UK that can be prepared in a slow cooker can be found in this book. You can use a slow cooker or any other electric appliance that can basically cook the food slowly and steadily over a long time period. First, though, let's get some background on the slow cooker itself before we get to the recipes.

Chapter 1: What is Slow Cooker and How to Use it?

So, what exactly is a slow cooker, and who would want to use one? To be honest, it's one of the most basic appliances in your kitchen. It may also be the one that gets the most use if you know how to use it properly, which you will after reading this book.

A slow cooker accomplishes this with just two settings, high and low. It works its magic by slowly and steadily transforming the ingredients you throw into the pot into a delicious meal. In fact, even the high setting isn't that hot; it's closer to 300°, which is quite low compared to typical oven settings. Have you ever preheated your oven to 300 degrees Fahrenheit? Isn't it rare, if ever? However, this is where the slow cooker excels. It works by heating foods at a low temperature for an extended period of time, producing tender meats, flavorful vegetables, or delectable dishes as a result of all those aromas being trapped in that pot for hours at a time.

Who has time to wait eight hours for dinner? Everybody, including you. You've been working all day, right? If this is the case, you are the person for whom the slow cooker was created. In contrast to traditional cooking, which requires you to spend an hour or more in the kitchen preparing your meal, the slow cooker works while you do. Simply start it in the morning, and your dinner will be ready when you get home. No more coming home from a long day and wondering what to make for dinner. You can eat right away and then spend the rest of the evening doing whatever you want. You won't even have to do many dishes because your meal is mostly prepared in one pot.

1.1 How Do You Choose the Best Slow Cooker?

Are you still undecided about which slow cooker to purchase? Almost every slow cooker provides the same cooking programs, and they may appear similar to you, but there are several factors that distinguish a good slow cooker from a bad one, and here's how to find them:

Let's start with the basics: the size and shape of the slow cooker, which appear to be the most important factors. You can choose any of the slow cooker sizes available, ranging from 2 to 10 quarts, based on your usual serving size. A 2-3-quart slow cooker can cook enough food for two people at once. Slow cookers with oval shapes are better suited to holding all types of meat cuts and poultry.

The cooking mechanism and its programs are the next important considerations. It is best to purchase a slow cooker that not only has a SLOW COOK option but also one that allows you to SEAR your food. This will save you the trouble of switching the pots. And if you can find a slow cooker with a KEEP WARM function, that will be a huge help.

Finally, buy slow cookers with ceramic or porcelain crock pots because they are nonsticky and easy to clean. Also, look for slow cookers with see-through glass lids, which allow you to check on the food without having to open the lid repeatedly.

1.2 How to Slow Cook?

Although slow cooking appears to be a simple task, it does necessitate a basic understanding of how a slow cooker works. There are several guidelines that must be followed when using an electric slow cooker. A few simple steps can help you cook more efficiently and effectively. To achieve the desired result, a basic understanding of the device, its mechanism, and its control settings are required. Slow cookers, unlike

pressure cookers, do not need to maintain pressure. Temperature and time are the only underlying variables. You can call it a day once they're both in place. However, there are a number of other well-known benefits to using a slow cooker that will assist you in making your decision.

A slow cooker is very easy to use. Simply plug in your slow cooker, add the ingredients for your chosen meal, adjust the temperature to low or high as directed by the recipe, cover, and cook. After your meal is finished cooking, turn off the slow cooker to turn off the heating element, or keep it warm if you aren't ready to eat it yet. This brings us to the conclusion of our discussion.

1. Configure the Appliance

To begin, place the device on a stable surface near the power supply. Before connecting it, make sure it's completely clean from the inside out. If not, wipe it away with a soft dry towel. Rinse the inside of the pot with clean water. Ensure the cooking pot is clean before replacing it in the base unit. Make sure the base is completely dry from the outside before reassembling everything.

2. Connect and Start

It's almost time to plug in the appliance. If the recipe calls for preheating the liquid, pour it into the slow cooker and cover it with the lid. If you select the "Slow Cook" setting from the control panel, the display will show a fixed time and temperature. You can customize the settings by using the Temp and Time adjustment keys.

3. Putting Everything Together

Place all of the ingredients inside the cooking insert and keep the liquid level below the maximum limit to avoid spillage. When cooking, avoid adding food because it will produce a lot of froth.

4. Cover with the Lid

After adding the food, cover the lid and secure it in the grooves of the base unit. It is recommended that the lid be kept closed while the food is cooking inside. Lift it up only once every 30-60 minutes to stir the food.

5. Wait and See

When you choose a heat setting from LOW, MED, or HI, the cooking pot inside the slow cooker will begin to heat up in a few seconds and cook the meal steadily. You can relax and wait for it to finish while it is running. The food will then be cooked automatically.

6. Continue to Clean

After each cooking session, remember to clean the cooking pot. Because the inside pot is washable, it is simple to clean underwater. In contrast, the metallic housing should only be cleaned using a soft cloth. It's also a smart idea to wash the lid after each session.

1.3 Slow Cooker Safety Recommendations

- Cooking dry beans, lentils, or legumes in the slow cooker is not recommended. Soak them in water for at least 2-4 hours before cooking in a slow cooker with plenty of liquid.

- Thaw frozen foods before adding them to the slow cooker.

- Never leave food in a slow cooker for more than 8 hours at high heat without checking it.

- The slow cooker insert should not be kept in the refrigerator or freezer.

- Use a food thermometer to determine whether the meat is fully cooked and has reached the proper temperature.

Chapter 2: Benefits and Tips and Tricks of Slow Cooking

Coming home to a tasty, home-cooked meal is the ideal way to end a long day of work or errands. Fortunately, using your slow cooker makes this simple. Lunch and dinner can be prepared without using your hands. They require some forethought, but there's something magical about setting it, forgetting about it, and returning home to a hot, home-cooked meal. Slow cookers are freestanding cooking appliances that cook food at a low and consistent temperature, similar to braising in a Dutch oven. Although most slow-cooked dishes are liquid, such as chicken soup, or saucy, such as BBQ jackfruit, a little liquid is required to keep the bottom from burning.

2.1 Benefits of Slow Cooking

Two words come to mind when we think of an electric slow cooker as a modern high-tech cooking machine: convenience and simplicity. The ability to cook for a lengthy period of time while food is left unattended is not the only obvious advantage of using a slow cooker; there are several other benefits as well.

1. Hands-Free Cooking

Slow cookers, unlike other appliances, permit you to pre-cook your additives and then leave them to prepare on their own, which is a fantastic feature because it permits you to concentrate on other tasks while your meal cooks. To use a slow cooker, you simply need to add ingredients, choose the right settings, and walk away while it does all the hard work for you. This feature is very helpful for people who have busy schedules and don't have a lot of time to spend cooking dinner.

2. Added Flavor

Slow cookers are well-known for enhancing the flavor of a dish. It combines the numerous qualities of the ingredients used, resulting in a burst of aromas and additive-free, authentic flavors. Because the ingredients simmer at such low temp, a slow cooker permits for proper flavor distribution, resulting in a delectable dish.

3. Meat Tenderizes Easily

With a slow cooker at your disposal, you can quickly tenderize cheap cuts or tough meats, leaving them seamless and flavorful after a long process of cooking, which is why many venison meals are prepared in this manner. Less expensive cuts of beef, such as chuck steaks and roasts, can be made tender using a slow cooker.

4. Simple to Apply

You don't need much cooking or electrical appliance experience to use a slow cooker. All that remains is to toss everything into the slow cooker, choose your favored options, and turn it on. Even if you've never used a slow cooker before, you can create a culinary masterpiece because it's simple to use. It is enough to read the manual for user to be fully prepared to prepare a delicacy using this useful culinary device. A slow cooker recipe book is extremely helpful for beginners.

5. Prepare Healthy Meals

High heat is known to degrade nutrients in foods, lowering the overall nutrition value of a dish. High temperatures have been linked to the release of potentially toxic chemical compounds, which can even lead to kidney problems & even diabetes. Slow cooking preserves nutrients while preventing the formation of unwanted, potentially toxic compounds due to the extremely low temperatures used. Because you will not be cooking at high temperatures as you would when boiling or frying, when you employ a slow cooker, you can rest assured that your food won't overcook.

6. In the Long Run, Save Money

Slow cookers use lesser energy than a standard electric oven, allowing you to save much more money over time. Although using a slow cooker to make all meals is unrealistic, it can aid you to save money on expenses that would otherwise be incurred if you used other food preparation equipment. Because slow cookers are typically used to make large quantities of food, you may be able to save money on energy that would otherwise be spent on preparing individual meals. Slow cooker food is commonly served in many services, allowing you to save money on materials.

7. Simple to Keep Up

Low cooking temperatures, as opposed to using an electric oven, reduce the likelihood of food sticking to the bottom. You'll also appreciate the fact that cooking with a slow cooker requires fewer utensils to be washed.

8. Various Types Are Available

Slow cookers have become more versatile as technology has advanced, with some even having pre-programmed settings. Slow cookers with basic settings like medium, hot, keep warm, or low must be turned off and on manually. Electronic timers found in today's slow cookers make it possible for the appliance to multitask while you cook, and a wide range of settings means that you can make your food just the way you like it.

9. Serve with Reheating

It takes longer for slow-cooked food to cool fully. Even much better, most new slow cookers have 'stay warm' settings that keep your meal warm after it's cooked.

2.2 Slow Cooker Tips and Tricks

To save time and effort during hectic days, it can be tempting to grab a quick meal from a drive-thru. However, if you use a slow cooker, you can omit those steps entirely. Dinner will be even more enjoyable with these suggestions for using a slow cooker.

1. Invest in Quality Cuts of Meat

It's a common situation: you wanted to make a dish but didn't have the type of meat called for in the recipe, so you used something else. You overcooked it, so the pork roast was hard and dry and greasy. When cooking at a low temperature for a long time, the best results are achieved with well-marbled cuts. There's no better time to make the most of cheaper cuts of meat like pork shoulder, beef chuck roast, and chicken thighs. Trim meats before trying to cook or prepare to remove some fat prior to serving to reduce grease.

2. It's Best to Start by Searing the Meat

There's something you need to know before you throw a raw roast into the slow cooker. The meat will have more flavor, and its delicious juices will be preserved if you brown it ahead of time. To further enhance the meat's taste, try adding a rub or spice mixture. There will be a huge difference after taking these few minutes to do this.

3. Make Sure the Slow Cooker Doesn't Get Too Full

Your slow cooker has started shaking halfway through cooking. As it happens, the crock's contents are bubbling over, which is why the lid is banging against the crock. Once you open the slow cooker to serve dinner, the food might be a solid lump or it might have evaporated altogether. Eek! Make absolutely sure your recipe fits the slow cooker's ideal fill level of between half and three-quarters. Altering cooking times may be necessary if more or less food is being prepared.

4. Roughly Chop Vegetables to the Same Size

All day long, we've been able to smell that slow cooker full of beef stew. But when you take a bite, you may find that some of the vegetables are crunchy and not even crisp-tender, while others have completely vanished. That's why it's crucial to properly prep your vegetables to avoid this sort of misfortune. To ensure uniform cooking, they must all be of similar size.

5. No Peeking!

You're craving Slow-Cooker Barbacoa, but please don't go looking for it. It will take much longer to prepare your food if you keep opening the lid and letting the heat escape (And remember to purchase a high-quality meat thermometer.)

6. Bear the Edges in Mind

Don't risk having parts of your much-anticipated lasagna recipe burn when you remove it from the cooker. It's fine to check the sides of "solid" foods like bread pudding, meat loaves, lasagna, and breakfast bakes for over-browning while they're cooking. Most slow cookers have a faster cooking zone on the side opposite the control panel, so that's where you should look first. To avoid burning your food, check on it quickly and only at the very end of the cooking time.

7. Make the Sauce Thicker

Don't waste the broth from tonight's slow-cooked chicken recipe by throwing it away. Because the lid is always on a slow cooker, none of the juices can escape. They may turn out thinner or more numerous than you prefer as a result. Move them to a saucepan and use flour or cornstarch to make a gravy.

8. Always Integrate Cheese in the Last

Personally, we think we can all relate to this. In your haste to make a delicious dish in the slow cooker, you may have overcooked the cheese on top and the dish altogether. A gummy, rubbery mess is the worst possible scenario. You need not give up cheese altogether to avoid this problem. The key is to remember to add it at the end, about 5 to 10 minutes prior to serving.

9. Do Not Overcook

You could be overcooking your recipes if your family regularly complains about the chalky meat, mushy vegetables, and muddy, one-note flavors in your slow-cooked meals. When you need to keep something cooking for longer than the recipe calls for, use the "Keep Warm" function of your slow cooker.

10. Putting Off the Dishwashing

Cleanup after using a slow cooker is by far the most unrewarding aspect of using one. It's something nobody enjoys doing, but it's something that must be done. That's not quite right. As a result of using a slow cooker liner, you can skip most of the dishwashing and get right to enjoying your slow-cooked, tender meal.

11. Don't Limit Yourself

To those who believe that slow cookers are only useful for making stew, we have some news for you. Rice pudding, mulled wine, and cheesecake are all possible to prepare. If you're in need of some ideas, take a look at the wide variety of dishes that can be prepared inside a slow cooker.

Chapter 3: Maintaining and Cleaning the Slow Cooker

If they aren't properly cleaned and maintained, even the best kitchen appliances can cause a lot of hassle. Electric cooking appliances need regular cleaning and maintenance to work well and last as long as possible. Several precautions and guidelines should be taken into account before you begin using a slow cooker for the first time.

- Allow the slow cooker to cool after you've finished using it.

- Remove the cooking insert or pot from the cooker and rinse with soapy water.

- You can also clean its insert in the dishwasher and then thoroughly dry it before replacing it.

- Then, wash and clean the slow cooker lid.

- The base unit should not be submerged in water or rinsed underwater. Simply wipe

it down with a cloth to clean it. And the inner pot can be hand-washed or washed in the dishwasher. Replace the insert in its original location once it has dried completely.

- Before each cooking session, spray the walls of the cooking pot with nonstick cooking spray.

- Do not put the frozen poultry and meat straight into the pot. It should be thawed in the refrigerator first before cooking. Avoid using frozen meat at all costs. Add extra cooking time to the total cooking time if you are not thawing the meat.

- In the inner pot, the cooking container should be no more than two-thirds complete and no less than half full. The cooking time is affected by the amount of food. As a result, it should not go above or below the allowed limits.

Tips on Cleaning the Slow Cooker

If you want your slow cooker to perform at its best, you need to treat it like every other kitchen appliance and clean it regularly. Slow cookers should be turned off, unplugged from the wall, and allowed to cool before cleaning. Stoneware with removable lids and glass can be washed in soapy hot water or put in the dishwasher to be thoroughly cleaned. If you prefer to clean by hand, remember to do so in the following ways:

- Avoid using harsh chemicals or scouring pads. Use sponges, rags, or even a rubber spatula to scrub away grime.

- In order to get rid of spots and stains, you should use vinegar or a nonabrasive cleaner.

- Never put hot stoneware in the dishwasher.

- The heating base must never be submerged in liquid.

A Deep Clean for Your Slow Cooker: An Extra Bonus Tip

Just like you've been meaning to clean out that cluttered closet, your slow cooker also needs a thorough cleaning from time to time. This recipe for a deep clean of your slow cooker will have it looking like new in no time, and it's the perfect task for a day of spring cleaning.

- The water level in your slow cooker should reach just above the highest level of any discarded food.

- If using a slow cooker that holds 3 quarts, add 1/2 cup of white vinegar; if using a slow cooker that holds 6 quarts, use 1 cup of vinegar.

- To a 3-quart slow cooker, slowly add 1/2 cup of baking soda; a 6-quart slow cooker will need 1 cup. Wait for the foam to subside before adding more.

- Cover, and cook on LOW for 1 hour.

- After the hour is up, take off the lid and clean with a damp sponge and some elbow grease, if necessary.

- After it has cooled, remove the inner pot and wash it in warm, soapy water in the sink.

- You can dry it off by placing it on the counter.

Maintaining the Peak Performance of Your Slow Cooker

Your slow cooker has served your family well for many years and deserves the best of care in return for all the delicious meals, good times, and happy memories it has given you. Natural wear and tear will eventually show up in your stoneware, removable lid, or slow cooker, no matter how often you scrub it.

Avoiding Mess

Finally, Slow Cooker Liners can help with much less mess during use. These liners are particularly useful for quick cleanup; simply toss the mess away! After that, a light cleaning after every use will aid in keeping your slow cooker in top condition.

Chapter 4: Slow Cooker Recipes

Breakfast

1. Oatmeal with Berry

Preparation time: 15 minutes | **Cooking time:** 4 to 6 hours | **Servings:** 2

Nutritional Value: Calories 368 | Total Fat 7g | Protein 9g | Carbs 68g | Sodium 97mg | Fiber 6g | Sugar 33g

Ingredients:

- 95 g of dried blueberries
- 150 ml of almond milk
- 500 g of rolled oats
- ¼ tsp. of ground cinnamon
- 1 egg
- 1 tbsp. of melted coconut oil
- 40 ml of honey
- 95 g of dried cherries
- ¼ tsp. of salt
- ¼ tsp. of ground ginger

Instructions:

- Apply a small amount of vegetable oil to the inside of a 6-quart slow cooker using a small brush.
- Fill the slow cooker halfway with oatmeal.
- Inside a medium mixing bowl, combine the eggs, almond milk, cinnamon, coconut oil, honey, salt, and ginger. Mix until completely combined. Pour the oats inside the slow cooker with this mixture.
- Dried blueberries and dried cherries should be sprinkled on top. Put the lid back on.
- Cook for around 4 to 6 hours on low heat or till the oatmeal combination is set and the edges begin to turn yellow.

2. Cheesy Ham Casserole

Preparation time: 10 minutes | **Cooking time:** 8 hours | **Servings:** 2

Nutritional Value: Calories 324 | Total Fat 8g | Protein 27g | Carbs 19g | Sodium 866mg | Fiber 5g | Sugar 1g

Ingredients:

- 2 slices of whole-grain bread, crusts removed, cut into one-inch cubes
- 1 tsp. of butter at room temperature
- Freshly ground black pepper

- 2 eggs

- 60 g of aged ham, diced

- 2 egg whites

- 60 g of hard cheese, such as Parmesan, shredded

Instructions:

- Grease the interior of the slow cooker using the butter.

- Inside a small-sized bowl, whisk together the eggs, egg white, and a few grinds of black pepper.

- Place the ham, bread, and cheese inside the slow cooker. Pour the egg mixture over the top and gently stir to combine.

- Cook, covered, on low for around 8 hours or overnight.

---

3. Peppers Stuffed with Sausage, Egg and Cheese

Preparation time: 10 minutes | **Cooking time:** 4 to 5 hours | **Servings:** 2

Nutritional Value: Calories 450 | Total Fat 36g | Protein 25g | Carbs 8g | Sodium 123mg | Fiber 3g | Sugar 4g

Ingredients:

- ½ tsp. of freshly ground black pepper

- 1 tbsp. of extra-virgin olive oil

- 120 g of shredded Cheddar Cheese

- 2 bell peppers, tops cut off and seeds discarded

- 170 g of breakfast sausage, crumbled

- 60 ml of coconut milk

- 3 eggs

- 1 scallion, white & green parts, chopped

Instructions:

- Line a slow cooker insert with foil and grease it using olive oil.

- Fill two peppers evenly with sausage crumbles and place them inside the slow cooker.

- Inside a medium-sized mixing bowl, combine the coconut milk, pepper, eggs, and scallions. Pour the egg mixture over the peppers. Then, cover them with the cheese.

- Cook on low for around 4 to 5 hours or till the eggs are set.

---

4. Vanilla Quinoa and Fruit Breakfast

Preparation time: 10 minutes | **Cooking time:** 8 hours | **Servings:** 2

Nutritional Value: Calories 323 | Total Fat 1g | Protein 11g | Carbs 53g | Sodium 122mg | Fiber 8g | Sugar 4g

Ingredients:

- 1 tsp. of vanilla extract

- 500 g of fresh fruit

- 96 g of quinoa

- 720 ml water

- ⅛ tsp. of sea salt

- 2 tbsps. of toasted pecans for garnish

Instructions:

- Add the quinoa, fruit, and salt to the slow cooker. Mix in the water and vanilla extract till thoroughly combined.

- Cook, covered, on low for around 8 hours or overnight.

- Serve with a sprinkle of toasted pecans on top.

5. Vanilla Cinnamon Pumpkin Pudding

Preparation time: 10 minutes | **Cooking time:** 6 to 7 hours | **Servings:** 2

Nutritional Value: Calories 265 | Total Fat 22g | Protein 13g | Carbs 8g | Sodium 121mg | Fiber 3g | Sugar 7g

Ingredients:

- ¼ tsp. of ground cinnamon

- 20 g of melted butter divided

- 250 ml of canned pumpkin purée

- 2 eggs

- ½ tbsp. of pure vanilla extract

- 180 ml of coconut milk

- 50 g of granulated erythritol

- Pinch of ground cloves

- ¼ tsp. of baking powder

- 20 g of protein powder

- 50 g of almond flour

- ¼ tsp. of ground nutmeg

Instructions:

- 1 tablespoon of butter should be used to lightly grease the slow cooker insert.

- Inside a large-sized mixing bowl, combine the remaining butter, eggs, coconut milk, pumpkin, and vanilla extract. Whisk until well combined.

- Inside a small-sized bowl, combine the erythritol, protein powder, almond flour, nutmeg, baking powder, cinnamon, and cloves.

- Combine the dry and wet ingredients.

- Fill the insert with the mixture.

- Cook on low for around 6 to 7 hours, covered.

- Serve warm.

6. Slow Cooker Vanilla Pumpkin and Pecan Oatmeal

Preparation time: 10 minutes | **Cooking time:** 8 hours | **Servings:** 2

Nutritional Value: Calories 292 | Total Fat 26g | Protein 10g | Carbs 9g | Sodium 92mg | Fiber 2g | Sugar 11g

Ingredients:

- 1 tbsp. of coconut oil
- ¼ tsp. of ground cinnamon
- 225 ml coconut milk
- 2 cubed pumpkins, cut into one-inch chunks
- 50 g of ground pecans
- 1 tbsp. of granulated erythritol
- 15 g of plain protein powder
- ¼ tsp. of ground nutmeg
- 1 tsp. of maple extract
- Pinch of ground allspice

Instructions:

- Lightly coat the insert of a slow cooker using coconut oil.
- Add the coconut milk, nutmeg, pumpkin, protein powder, cinnamon, pecans, erythritol, maple extract, and allspice to the slow cooker insert.
- Cook for around 8 hours on low, covered.
- Serve after thoroughly stirring the mixture or creating your desired texture using a potato masher.

7. Layered Vegetable Cheese and Egg Casserole

Preparation time: 10 minutes | **Cooking time:** 4 hours | **Servings:** 2

Nutritional Value: Calories 338 | Total Fat 29g | Protein 18g | Carbs 2g | Sodium 285mg | Fiber 0g | Sugar 1g

Ingredients:

- ½ zucchini, chopped
- ½ tbsp. of extra-virgin olive oil
- 160 g of shredded Cheddar Cheese
- 150 g of breakfast sausage
- ½ tsp. freshly ground black pepper
- ½ sweet onion, chopped
- 3 eggs
- ½ red bell pepper, finely chopped
- 100 ml of heavy (whipping) cream
- ½ tsp. of salt

Instructions:

- Lightly coat the slow cooker insert using olive oil.
- Arrange half of the sausage in the bottom of the insert, and on top of the sausage, layer half of the zucchini, pepper, and onion. After that, sprinkle half of the cheese over the vegetables. Repeat to add another layer.
- Inside a medium-sized mixing bowl, combine the heavy cream, salt, eggs, and pepper. Pour the egg mixture over the casserole.
- Cook for 4 hours on low, covered.

- Serve hot.

8. Creamy Mashed Potatoes

Preparation time: 15 minutes | **Cooking time:** 2 to 3 hours | **Servings:** 2

Nutritional Value: Calories 299 | Total Fat 20g | Protein 6g | Carbs 25g | Sodium 390mg | Fiber 1g | Sugar 2g

Ingredients:

- 500 g of mashed potato flakes

- 160 ml of 2% milk

- 120 ml of cream cheese softened

- 200 ml of boiling water

- 1 tsp. of garlic salt

- 40 ml of butter, cubed

- ¼ tsp. of pepper

- Minced fresh parsley, optional

- 60 ml of sour cream

Instructions:

- Inside a greased 4-quart slow cooker, whisk together the milk, sour cream, butter, cream cheese, and boiling water till smooth. Stir in the garlic potato flakes, salt, and pepper.

- Cook on low for around 2 to 3 hours or till heated through. If desired, garnish using parsley.

9. Slow Cooker Spiced Pear Oatmeal

Preparation time: 10 minutes | **Cooking time:** 8 hours | **Servings:** 2

Nutritional Value: Calories 553 | Total Fat 13g | Protein 16g | Carbs 98g | Sodium 368mg | Fiber 19g | Sugar 43g

Ingredients:

- 150g of steel-cut oats

- ⅛ tsp. of ground ginger

- ¼ tsp. of cinnamon

- ⅛ tsp. of ground nutmeg

- ⅛ tsp. of sea salt

- 720 ml of unsweetened almond milk or water

- ⅛ tsp. of ground cardamom

- 1 ripe pear, peeled, cored, and diced

Instructions:

- Stir together the ginger, cardamom, nutmeg, cinnamon, oats, and salt in the slow cooker. Stir in the almond milk and pear.

- Cook the oatmeal on low for 8 hours or overnight, covered.

10. Garlicky Bacon Egg Casserole

Preparation time: 10 minutes | **Cooking time:** 5 to 6 hours | **Servings:** 2

Nutritional Value: Calories 526 | Total Fat 43g | Protein 32g | Carbs 3g | Sodium 42mg | Fiber 0g | Sugar 17g

Ingredients:

- 100 ml of coconut milk
- ½ tbsp. of bacon fat or extra-virgin olive oil
- ¼ sweet onion, chopped
- 3 eggs
- 150 g of bacon, chopped and cooked crisp
- ¼ tsp. of freshly ground black pepper
- 1 tsp. of minced garlic
- ⅛ tsp. of salt
- Pinch red pepper flakes

Instructions:

- Lightly coat the slow cooker insert with bacon fat or olive oil.
- Inside a medium-sized mixing bowl, combine the coconut milk, salt, eggs, bacon, onion, garlic, pepper, & red pepper flakes. Fill the slow cooker halfway with the mixture.
- Cook on low for around 5 to 6 hours, covered.
- Serve hot.

Pasta

1. Slow Cooker Mac and Cheese

Preparation time: 10 minutes | **Cooking time:** 3 hours | **Servings:** 2

Nutritional Value: Calories 432 | Total Fat 25g | Protein 18g | Carbs 34g | Sodium 524mg | Fiber 1g | Sugar 5g

Ingredients:

- 1 (250 g) package of grated Cheddar cheese divided

- 2 well-beaten eggs

- 1 (250 g) package of elbow macaroni

- Salt and ground black pepper to taste

- 1 pinch of paprika

- 1 (150 ml) can of evaporated milk

- 450 ml of whole milk

- 120 g of butter

- 1 (300 ml) can of the condensed Cheddar cheese soup

Instructions:

- Fill a large-sized pot halfway using lightly salted water & bring to the boil. Return to boil after adding the macaroni. Cook, uncovered, for 8 minutes or till pasta is tender but firm to the bite. Drain the pasta and place it in the slow cooker.

- Salt and pepper to taste after adding the butter to the pasta. Stir in about half of Cheddar cheese over the pasta.

- Inside a mixing bowl, combine eggs and evaporated milk till smooth; mix into pasta mixture.

- Inside a mixing bowl, combine milk and condensed soup till smooth; mix into pasta mixture. Sprinkle the remaining cheese over the pasta mixture and top with paprika.

- Cook for around 3 hours on low.

2. Slow Cooker Lasagna

Preparation time: 10 minutes | **Cooking time:** 6 hours | **Servings:** 2

Nutritional Value: Calories 446 | Total Fat 20g | Protein 31g | Carbs 36g | Sodium 720mg | Fiber 3g | Sugar 8g

Ingredients:

- 1 (236 ml) can of tomato sauce

- 110 g of shredded mozzarella cheese

- 1/2 medium chopped onion

- 1 tsp. of minced garlic

- 1 (60 ml) can of tomato paste

- 110 g of cottage cheese

- 1/2 kg of lean ground beef

- ½ tsp. of salt

- 1 (113 g) package of lasagna noodles

- 1/2 tsp. of dried oregano

- 85 g of grated Parmesan cheese

Instructions:

- Inside a large-sized skillet over medium flame, brown the ground beef with the garlic and onion. Stir in the tomato sauce, salt, tomato paste, and oregano till just combined and warmed through.

- Inside a large-sized mixing bowl, combine cottage cheese, mozzarella, and Parmesan.

- Layer the meat mixture in the bottom of your slow cooker. a double layer of the uncooked lasagna noodles, splitting them as needed to fit into the cooker. Place a portion of the cheese mixture on top of the noodles. Layer the noodles, sauce, & cheese till all of the ingredients are being used.

- Cook for around 4 to 6 hours on Low, covered.

3. Slow Cooker Creamy Pesto Chicken Pasta

Preparation time: 10 minutes | **Cooking time:** 5 hours | **Servings:** 2

Nutritional Value: Calories 832 | Total Fat 50g | Protein 50g | Carbs 46g | Sodium 875mg | Fiber 3g | Sugar 2g

Ingredients:

- 150 ml of chicken broth

- 1 (125 ml) jar of pesto

- 1/2 kg of boneless and skinless chicken breasts

- 1 (110 g) package of egg noodles

- 250 ml of water, or as required

- Salt & pepper to taste

- 60 ml of milk

- 125 ml of heavy whipping cream, divided

- 56 g of grated Parmesan-Asiago-Romano cheese

Instructions:

- Place the chicken inside a slow cooker set to High. Cover with broth and water. Season using salt & pepper to taste.

- Cook, covered, for around 3 hours, or till the chicken is no pinker on the inside.

- Take the chicken out of the slow cooker & shred it using a fork. Put the chicken back in the pot. Pour in one cup of cream and the whole jar of pesto.

- Cook for another hour on high.

- Inside the slow cooker, combine the egg noodles, remaining cream, and 3/4 of the grated cheese. Pour in the milk.

- Cook till the noodles are tender, approximately 1 hour more on High. If you want a thinner sauce, add more milk. Finish with the remaining cheese.

4. Cheesy Tortellini

Preparation time: 10 minutes | **Cooking time:** 7 hours | **Servings:** 2

Nutritional Value: Calories 468 | Total Fat 24g | Protein 27g | Carbs 35g | Sodium 978mg | Fiber 4g | Sugar 10g

Ingredients:

- 1 (175 ml) jar of marinara sauce

- ½ kg of ground beef

- 1 (5-ounces) package of fresh or refrigerated cheese tortellini

- 0.5 kg of Italian sausage, casings removed

- 85 g of shredded Cheddar cheese

- 1 (6 ounces) can of undrained and diced tomatoes

- 100 g of shredded mozzarella cheese

- 1 (56 g) can of sliced mushrooms

Instructions:

- Melt butter inside a large-sized skillet over medium-high flame. In a hot skillet, cook & stir Italian sausage and ground beef till crumbly and golden brown, approximately 10 minutes. Drain.

- Inside a slow cooker, combine marinara sauce, tomatoes, ground meats, and mushrooms. Cook on Low for around 7 to 8 hours, covered.

- Tortellini should be mixed into the marinara meat sauce. Top with Cheddar and mozzarella cheese. Cook, covered, on Low for around 15 minutes or till tortellini is tender.

5. Slow Cooker Chicken Tetrazzini

Preparation time: 10 minutes | **Cooking time:** 4 hours | **Servings:** 2

Nutritional Value: Calories 374 | Total Fat 26g | Protein 26g | Carbs 8g | Sodium 677mg | Fiber 0g | Sugar 3g

Ingredients:

- 1 (75 ml) can of condensed cream chicken soup

- 2 boneless and skinless chicken breast halves

- 1 (56 g) package of dry Italian-style salad dressing mix

- 60 ml of chicken broth

- 1 tbsp. of butter

- 1/2 small onion, sliced and made into rings

- 1 tbsp. of melted butter

- 3 cloves of minced garlic

- 1 (60 ml) package of softened cream cheese

Instructions:

- Place the chicken inside the slow cooker. Put 2 tablespoons of melted butter on top; sprinkle using Italian dressing mix.

- Cook for around 3 hours on High, covered.

- Inside a large-sized skillet over medium flame, melt the remaining two tablespoons of butter. Cook, stirring constantly, till the onion is soft, approximately 5 minutes. Combine the cream of chicken broth, chicken soup, and cream cheese. Inside the slow cooker, pour the mixture over the cooked chicken.

- Cook, covered, on Low for 1 hour or till the chicken is fork soft, and the sauce has thickened.

Rice and Whole-Grains

1. Spicy Quinoa

Preparation time: 10 minutes | **Cooking time:** 10 hours | **Servings:** 2

Nutritional Value: Calories 266 | Total Fat 7g | Protein 12g | Carbs 43g | Sodium 1044mg | Fiber 11g | Sugar 5g

Ingredients:

- 1 medium bell pepper (any color), seeded and diced
- 150 g of dried black beans, rinsed
- 1 large tomato, diced
- 67 g uncooked quinoa, rinsed
- 1 garlic clove, minced
- 85 g of chopped fresh cilantro
- 1 jalapeño, halved and seeded, optional
- 500 ml of water
- 200 ml of Vegetable Stock
- 1/2 tsp. of ground cumin
- 1 tsp. of chili powder
- Sea salt
- 1/2 medium onion, diced
- 1 dried chipotle
- Chopped avocado and lime wedges for the garnish

Instructions:

- Add the black beans, jalapenos, chipotles, tomatoes, onion, quinoa, garlic, bell peppers, stock, and water inside the slow cooker.
- Cook for around 10 hours on low or 5 hours on high in a covered slow cooker.
- After cooking, stir in the chili powder, cumin, and cilantro. Taste and season using salt as desired.
- Remove the chipotles and serve the quinoa with chopped avocado and a squeeze of lime.

2. Garlicky Rice with Peas

Preparation time: 10 minutes | **Cooking time:** 6 hours | **Servings:** 2

Nutritional Value: Calories 425 | Total Fat 9g | Protein 32g | Carbs 58g | Sodium 412mg | Fiber 7g | Sugar 3g

Ingredients:

- 250 g of long-grain white rice, uncooked

- ½ tsp. of dried basil leaves

- 1 minced garlic cloves

- 1/2 chopped onions

- 40 ml water

- 210 ml cans of reduced-sodium Chicken Broth

- ¾ tsp. of Italian seasoning

- 20 g of grated Parmesan cheese

- 125 g of frozen baby peas, thawed

Instructions:

- Mix the garlic, onions, and rice inside the slow cooker.

- Inside a saucepan, combine the chicken broth and water. Bring to the boil. Add the basil leaves and Italian Incorporate into the rice mixture.

- Cook on low for around 2 to 3 hours or till the liquid has been absorbed.

- Stir in the peas thoroughly. Cook for another 30 minutes, covered. Before serving, stir in the cheese after it has finished cooking.

3. Cranberry and Apricot Rice

Preparation time: 10 minutes | **Cooking time:** 2 hours | **Servings:** 2

Nutritional Value: Calories 303 | Total Fat 8g | Protein 24g | Carbs 33g | Sodium 217mg | Fiber 5g | Sugar 5g

Ingredients:

- 85 g of chopped dried apricots

- 85 g of dried cranberries

- 150 g of pkg. long-grain and wild rice mix

- 85 g of chopped onion

- 380 ml Chicken Broth

Instructions:

- Spray a small-sized frying pan using nonstick cooking spray. Cook, stirring occasionally, until the onions start to brown, approximately 5 minutes.

- Add the cooked onions and the remaining ingredients, along with the seasonings from the rice package, to the slow cooker. Seasonings should be thoroughly mixed in.

- Cook for around 2 hours on high with the lid on. After cooking, fluff using a fork before serving.

4. Slow Cooker Barley with Mushrooms

Preparation time: 20 minutes | **Cooking time:** 8 hours | **Servings:** 2

Nutritional Value: Calories 271 | Total Fat 10g | Protein 10g | Carbs 39g | Sodium 1092mg | Fiber 8g | Sugar 6g

Ingredients:

- 1/2 tbsp. of finely chopped garlic

- 85 g of diced celery

- 250 ml of water

- 500 ml of beef broth

- 125 ml of milk

- 85 g of chopped brown beech mushrooms

- 2 tbsps. olive oil

- 110g of diced onion

- 85 g of diced carrot

- 1 (85 g) package of sliced white mushrooms

- 1 (150 ml) can of condensed cream of mushroom soup

- 85 g of chopped oyster mushrooms

- 85 g of dried shiitake mushrooms

- ½ tsp. of ground mixed peppercorns

- 85 g of dried black mushrooms

- ½ teaspoon of salt

- 110 g of barley

Instructions:

- Inside a slow cooker set to High, heat the water; add the barley, salt, beef broth, milk, olive oil, garlic, onion, celery, carrot, black mushrooms, cream of mushroom soup, oyster mushrooms, white mushrooms, brown beech mushrooms, shiitake mushrooms, and ground mixed peppercorns.

- Cook for around 1 hour on High, covered.

- Using a slotted spoon, remove the shiitake mushrooms and chop them into 1/2-inch pieces. Reduce the setting to Low & cook for another 7 hours.

5. Barley with Sausage

Preparation time: 20 minutes | **Cooking time:** 8 hours | **Servings:** 2

Nutritional Value: Calories 382 | Total Fat 23g | Protein 21g | Carbs 23g | Sodium 722mg | Fiber 5g | Sugar 5g

Ingredients:

- 0.5 kg of Italian sausage

- 1 (141 g) package of frozen chopped spinach

- 85 g of diced onion

- ½ tsp. of Italian seasoning

- 85 g of uncooked pearl barley

- 1 (750 ml) can of chicken broth

- 1/2 tbsp. of minced garlic

- 1 large sliced carrot

Instructions:

- Inside a skillet over medium flame, brown the onion, sausage, and garlic until evenly brown. Season to taste with Italian seasoning. Remove from the flame and set aside to drain.

- Inside a slow cooker, combine the sausage mixture, spinach, carrot, chicken broth, and barley.

- Cook on High for around 4 hours or Low for around 6 to 8 hours, covered.

6. Herbed Rice with Almonds

Preparation time: 20 minutes | **Cooking time:** 6 hours | **Servings:** 2

Nutritional Value: Calories 70 | Total Fat 2g | Protein 1g | Carbs 23g | Sodium 610mg | Fiber 0.5g | Sugar 1g

Ingredients:

- 1/4 tsp. of dried marjoram

- 1 chicken bouillon cubes

- 320 ml of water

- 2 tbsps. of dried parsley, chopped

- 1/2 tbsp. of butter or margarine

- 200 g of long-grain rice, uncooked

- 1/2 tsp. of dried rosemary

- 24 g of slivered almonds, optional

- 1/4 onion, diced

Instructions:

- Combine the chicken bouillon cubes and water inside a mixing bowl, then pour into the slow cooker.

- Fill the slow cooker halfway with the remaining ingredients.

- Cook, covered, on low for around 4 to 6 hours or until the rice is tender.

7. Rice with Beans and Salsa

Preparation time: 20 minutes | **Cooking time:** 4 to 10 hours | **Servings:** 2

Nutritional Value: Calories 551 | Total Fat 7g | Protein 38g | Carbs 87g | Sodium 314mg | Fiber 4g | Sugar 3g

Ingredients:

- 110 g of long-grain white or brown rice, uncooked

- 1 can (200 g) Chicken Broth

- 140 ml of water

- 1 can (200 g) of black or navy beans, drained

- Salsa, your choice of heat

- ½ tsp. of garlic powder

Instructions:

- Combine all of the ingredients inside the slow cooker. Stir everything together thoroughly.

- Cook on low for around 8 to 10 hours or on high for around 4 hours, covered.

8. Three-Grain Medley

Preparation time: 20 minutes | **Cooking time:** 6 hours | **Servings:** 2

Nutritional Value: Calories 200 | Total Fat 8g | Protein 4g | Carbs 28g | Sodium 1030mg | Fiber 4g | Sugar 3g

Ingredients:

- 2 tbsps. of chopped fresh parsley
- 85 g of uncooked wheat berries
- 1 clove of garlic, finely chopped
- 85 g of uncooked pearl or hulled barley
- 1 jar (28 g) of undrained diced pimientos
- 2 tbsps. of melted butter or oil
- 85 g of uncooked wild rice
- 1 tsp. of finely shredded lemon peel
- 2 medium-sized green onions, thinly sliced (2 tbsps.)
- 1 can (207 ml) of vegetable broth

Instructions:

- Inside a 3-1/2- to 6-quart slow cooker, combine all of the ingredients.
- Cook for around 4 to 6 hours on a Low setting, or till liquid is soaked up. Before serving, give it a good stir.

9. Quinoa Hot Cereal with Cranberry

Preparation time: 20 minutes | **Cooking time:** 6 to 8 hours | **Servings:** 2

Nutritional Value: Calories 284 | Total Fat 4g | Protein 4g | Carbs 28g | Sodium 1030mg | Fiber 4g | Sugar 3g

Ingredients:

- 250 g of quinoa, drained and rinsed
- 1/2 tsp. of ground cinnamon
- 180 ml of unsweetened apple juice
- 270 ml of water
- 1/4 tsp. of vanilla extract
- 60 ml of honey
- 500 ml of canned coconut milk
- 250 g of dried cranberries
- ½ tsp. of salt

Instructions:

- Inside a 6-quart slow cooker, combine all of the ingredients and gently stir using a spoon. Cook on low for around 6 to 8 hours or till the quinoa is creamy and tender.
- Move the mixture from the pot to the bowl using a spoon & serve!

10. Slow Cooker Rice with Chicken

Preparation time: 20 minutes | **Cooking time:** 3 hours | **Servings:** 2

Nutritional Value: Calories 316 | Total Fat 2g | Protein 17g | Carbs 54g | Sodium 1589mg | Fiber 4g | Sugar 9g

Ingredients:

- 1/2 chopped small onion

- 1 (283 g) can of diced tomatoes, undrained

- 1 large coarsely chopped bell pepper

- 170 g of uncooked long-grain white rice

- 250 ml of water

- 1/2 tsp. of cayenne pepper

- 1 (1/1 ounce) package of taco seasoning mix

- 1/2 tsp. of salt

- 1 skinless & boneless chicken breast cut into one-inch pieces

- 1/2 tsp. of ground black pepper

Instructions:

- Inside a slow cooker, combine pepper, tomatoes, water, bell peppers, rice, onion, chicken, taco seasoning, salt, and cayenne; stir to combine. Cook for around 6 to 8 hours on low or around 3 to 4 hours on high.

Salads and Sauces

1. Slow Cooker Spiced Applesauce

Preparation time: 20 minutes | **Cooking time:** 6 hours | **Servings:** 2

Nutritional Value: Calories 151 | Total Fat 0g | Protein 0g | Carbs 39g | Sodium 8mg | Fiber 3g | Sugar 34g

Ingredients:

- 85 g of packed brown sugar
- 2 apples - cored, peeled, and thinly sliced
- 1/2 tsp. of pumpkin pie spice
- 125 ml of water

Instructions:

- Inside a slow cooker, combine apples and water; cook on Low for around 6 to 8 hours. Cook for another 30 minutes after adding pumpkin pie spice and brown sugar.

2. Slow Cooker Tomato Sauce

Preparation time: 10 minutes | **Cooking time:** 10 hours | **Servings:** 2

Nutritional Value: Calories 105 | Total Fat 9g | Protein 1g | Carbs 6g | Sodium 394mg | Fiber 2g | Sugar 3g

Ingredients:

- 1/2 tsp. of minced garlic
- 4 Roma (plum) tomatoes ~ seeded, peeled and crushed
- 1/4 chopped small onion
- 1/2 tsp. of dried basil
- 2 tbsps. of olive oil
- 1/2 tsp. of salt
- 1/2 tsp. of dried oregano
- 1/2 tsp. of ground cayenne pepper
- 1 pinch of cinnamon
- 1/2 tsp. of ground black pepper

Instructions:

- Inside a slow cooker, combine tomatoes, black pepper, onion, salt, garlic, and olive oil. Add oregano, cayenne pepper, basil, and cinnamon to taste.
- Cook on Low for around 10 to 15 hours, covered. The longer you leave it to simmer, the tastier it becomes. It's excellent at 10 hours, but even better at 15.

3. Slow Cooker Steak Salad with Lime Cilantro Dressing

Preparation time: 20 minutes | **Cooking time:** 8 hours | **Servings:** 2

Nutritional Value: Calories 278 | Total Fat 19g | Protein 17g | Carbs 13g | Sodium 421mg | Fiber 5g | Sugar 3g

Ingredients:

- 1 tbsp. of olive oil
- 0.5 kg of beef skirt steak
- 1/2 tbsp. of steak seasoning

For salad:

- 1/2 large diced avocado
- 1 ear of corn, kernels cut out from the cob
- 2 mini sweet peppers, sliced
- 1 head of romaine, chopped
- 110 g of grape tomatoes, sliced

For dressing:

- 2 tbsps. of chopped fresh cilantro
- Salt to taste
- 60 ml of Greek yogurt
- 1 tbsp. of lime juice

Instructions:

- Rub olive oil & steak seasoning over the steak. Cover and place inside a slow cooker. Cook on Low for around 8 hours or till the potatoes are tender.

- Remove the steak and set it aside to cool slightly. Forks can be used to slice or shred the meat.

- Inside a large mixing bowl, combine corn, romaine, mini peppers, avocado, and tomatoes.

- Inside a food processor or blender, combine yogurt, lime juice, cilantro, and salt till smooth.

- Drizzle dressing over the steak pieces in the salad.

4. Cranberry Sauce

Preparation time: 20 minutes | **Cooking time:** 3 hours | **Servings:** 2

Nutritional Value: Calories 85 | Total Fat 0g | Protein 0g | Carbs 22g | Sodium 4mg | Fiber 1g | Sugar 19g

Ingredients:

- 2 tbsps. of orange juice
- 85 g of white sugar
- 60 ml of water
- 42 g of brown sugar
- 1 (110 g) package of the fresh cranberries
- Pinch of ground cinnamon

Instructions:

- Inside a slow cooker, combine white sugar, orange juice, brown sugar, water, and cinnamon; stir in cranberries. Cook for around 3 hours on High, stirring once an hour.

- Remove the lid and thoroughly stir. Cook for around 45 minutes on High or till the sauce has distended and most of the cranberries have popped.

5. Quinoa Salad with Feta and Arugula

Preparation time: 20 minutes | **Cooking time:** 3 hours | **Servings:** 2

Nutritional Value: Calories 352 | Total Fat 13g | Protein 12g | Carbs 46g | Sodium 575mg | Fiber 7g | Sugar 5g

Ingredients:

- 110 g of uncooked quinoa, rinsed

- 1/4 tsp. of kosher salt

- 85 g of chopped and drained roasted red bell peppers

- 250 ml of unsalted vegetable stock

- 1 (198 g) can of no-salt-added chickpeas, rinsed and drained

- 110 g of sliced red onions (from 1 onion)

- 6 pitted Kalamata olives, lengthwise halved

- 1 clove of garlic, minced

- 1 tbsp. of olive oil

- 28 g of feta cheese, crumbled

- 1 tsp. of fresh lemon juice

- 1 tbsp. of chopped fresh oregano

- 330 g of baby arugula

Instructions:

- Inside a five- to six-quart slow cooker, combine the stock, 1/2 tablespoon olive oil, quinoa, onions, chickpeas, garlic, and 1/2 teaspoon salt. Cook on LOW for 3 to 4 hours or till the quinoa is soft and the stock has been absorbed.

- Turn the slow cooker off. Using a fork, fluff the quinoa mixture. Combine the lemon juice, remaining 2 tablespoons of the olive oil, and 1/4 teaspoon salt in a mixing bowl. Toss the slow cooker with the olive oil mixture & red bell peppers to combine. Mix in the arugula gently. Cover and set aside for 10 minutes or till the arugula is mildly wilted. Sprinkle the feta cheese, olives, and oregano evenly over each serving.

Appetizers

1. Cheese Stuffed Jalapeño Peppers

Preparation time: 15 minutes | **Cooking time:** 4 hours | **Servings:** 2

Nutritional Value: Calories 352 | Total Fat 13g | Protein 5g | Carbs 3g | Sodium 176mg | Fiber 0.3g | Sugar 2g

Ingredients:

- 20 ml of sour cream

- 20 ml of Chicken Stock or water

- 4 jalapeños, washed, seeded, and halved lengthwise

- 100 ml of cream cheese at room temperature

- 6 slices of bacon

- 28 g of Cheddar cheese grated

Instructions:

- Inside a medium-sized mixing bowl, combine the cream cheese, sour cream, and grated Cheddar cheese until well combined.

- Divide the cheese mixture evenly among the jalapeno halves, and wrap each stuffed jalapeno half with a slice of bacon, then secure with a toothpick.

- Add the stuffed jalapenos to the slow cooker with the chicken stock.

- Cook for around 4 hours on low or around 2 hours on high in a covered slow cooker.

- Using a slotted spoon, remove the stuffed jalapenos from the slow cooker and serve hot or at room temperature.

2. Cheese and Mushrooms Meatballs

Preparation time: 15 minutes | **Cooking time:** 6 to 8 hours | **Servings:** 2

Nutritional Value: Calories 774 | Total Fat 35g | Protein 30g | Carbs 84g | Sodium 378mg | Fiber 6g | Sugar 17g

Ingredients:

- 1/2 kg bag of prepared meatballs

- 1 can (60 g) of button mushrooms

- 1/2 medium diced onion

- 175 ml jar of Cheese Whiz

- 1 can (100 ml) of cream of mushroom

Instructions:

- Inside a slow cooker, combine all of the ingredients.

- Cook on low for around 6 to 8 hours, covered.

- Serve as an appetizer.

3. Apple Crumble with Peach

Preparation time: 15 minutes | **Cooking time:** 4 to 5 hours | **Servings:** 2

Nutritional Value: Calories 547 | Total Fat 26g | Protein 10g | Carbs 75g | Sodium 378mg | Fiber 11g | Sugar 42g

Ingredients:

- 60 ml of coconut oil, melted

- 3 large Granny Smith apples, peeled & cut into chunks

- 50 g of coconut sugar

- 1 tbsp. honey

- 1/2 tbsp. of lemon juice

- 2 large peaches, peeled and sliced

- 68 g of almond flour

- 1/4 tsp. of ground cinnamon

- 240 g of quick-cooking oatmeal

- 85 g of slivered almonds

Instructions:

- Inside a 6-quart slow cooker, combine the apples, honey, peaches, and lemon juice.

- Inside a large-sized mixing bowl, combine the almond flour, coconut sugar, cinnamon, oatmeal, and almonds. Drizzle using melted coconut oil and stir till the mixture is loose.

- Drizzle the almond mixture over the fruit mixture.

- Cook on low for around 4 to 5 hours or till the fruit is soft and frothy with crumbs around the edges.

4. Honey Cranberry Stuffed Acorn Squash

Preparation time: 10 minutes | **Cooking time:** 5 to 6 hours | **Servings:** 2

Nutritional Value: Calories 145 | Total Fat 7g | Protein 2g | Carbs 22g | Sodium 111mg | Fiber 2g | Sugar 9g

Ingredients:

- 1 tbsp. of honey

- 1 Acorn squash

- 85 g of chopped pecan or walnuts

- 1 tbsp. of olive oil (not extra-virgin)

- 85 g of chopped dried cranberries

Instructions:

- Cut the squash in half. Extract the seeds and pulp from the center. Make quarters by cutting the halves in half again.

- Place the squash quarters, cut-side up, inside the slow cooker.

- Combine the olive oil, pecans, honey, and cranberries inside a small-sized bowl.

- Fill the center of every squash quarter with the pecan mixture. Season using salt and pepper. Cook on low for around 5 to 6 hours or till the squash is tender. Serve immediately.

- Season using garlic, pepper, and rosemary (or the salt, minced garlic, and pepper). Toss once more till the potatoes are evenly coated.

- Place the potatoes in the slow cooker. Cook for around 2 to 3 hours on High or 5 to 6 hours on Low or till the potatoes are tender but not mushy or dry.

5. Rosemary Garlic New Potatoes

Preparation time: 10 minutes | **Cooking time:** 2 to 6 hours | **Servings:** 2

Nutritional Value: Calories 102 | Total Fat 3g | Protein 2g | Carbs 18g | Sodium 321mg | Fiber 2g | Sugar 2g

Ingredients:

- 1 tsp. of garlic and pepper seasoning, or 1 large minced clove of garlic

- 280 g of new red potatoes, unpeeled

- ¼ tsp. of pepper

- 1/2 tbsp. of fresh chopped rosemary, or 1 tsp. of dried rosemary

- 1 tbsp. of olive oil

- ½ tsp. of salt

Instructions:

- If the potatoes are larger than golf balls, cut them in half or quarters.

- Inside a bowl or plastic bag, coat potatoes thoroughly with olive oil.

Side Dishes

1. Slow Cooker Savory Root Vegetables

Preparation time: 10 minutes | **Cooking time:** 6 to 8 hours | **Servings:** 2

Nutritional Value: Calories 214 | Total Fat 5g | Protein 4g | Carbs 40g | Sodium 201mg | Fiber 6g | Sugar 7g

Ingredients:

- 2 carrots, cut into one-inch chunks
- 1 sweet potato, peeled and cut into chunks
- 2 Yukon Gold potatoes, cut into chunks
- 1 tbsp. of olive oil
- 2 whole garlic cloves, peeled
- 1 parsnip, peeled and cut into chunks
- ½ tsp. of salt
- 1 yellow onion, each cut into 8 wedges

- 1/2 tsp. of dried thyme leaves
- ⅛ tsp. of freshly ground black pepper

Instructions:

- Put everything in a slow cooker with a 6-quart capacity and close the lid. Cook the vegetables on low for around 6 to 8 hours or till they are soft. Serve right away.
- If you can't eat it all, you can store it in the fridge for up to a week.

2. Butter Glazed Sweet Potatoes

Preparation time: 10 minutes | **Cooking time:** 3 to 4 hours | **Servings:** 2

Nutritional Value: Calories 178 | Total Fat 3g | Protein 2g | Carbs 39g | Sodium 345mg | Fiber 1g | Sugar 4g

Ingredients:

- 1/2 tbsp. of flour
- 2 medium sweet potatoes
- 1/4 tsp. of salt
- 1 tbsp. of butter
- 20 ml of water
- 85 g of brown sugar

Instructions:

- Cook till the sweet potatoes are barely soft inside a large-sized saucepan with 2-3 inches of water. Drain. Peel and slice into the slow cooker when cool enough to handle.

- While the potatoes are cooking inside the saucepan, combine all of the remaining ingredients in a microwave-safe bowl.

- Microwave for 11/2 minutes on High. Repeat till the glaze has thickened slightly.

- In the slow cooker, pour the glaze over the peeled and cooked sweet potatoes.

- Cook for around 3 to 4 hours on high with the lid on.

3. Onion, Apples and Butternut Squash

Preparation time: 15 minutes | **Cooking time:** 4 hours | **Servings:** 2

Nutritional Value: Calories 71 | Total Fat 1g | Protein 2g | Carbs 16g | Sodium 5mg | Fiber 4g | Sugar 10g

Ingredients:

- 1/2 sweet yellow onion like Vidalia, sliced thin

- 2 cooking apples (Granny Smith or Honeycrisp work well), cored, peeled, and chopped

- 1/2 tsp. of ground nutmeg

- 1/2 (1/2 kg) butternut squash, seeded, peeled, and cubed

- A pinch of ground cinnamon

- 170 g of dried currants

Instructions:

- Add the apples, squash, onion, and currants to the slow cooker. Season using nutmeg and cinnamon.

- Cook for around 4 hours on high or till the squash is soft and cooked through. While cooking, stir occasionally.

4. Spiced Apple and Potato Stuffed Cabbage

Preparation time: 15 minutes | **Cooking time:** 4 hours | **Servings:** 2

Nutritional Value: Calories 120 | Total Fat 1g | Protein 4g | Carbs 128g | Sodium 135mg | Fiber 5g | Sugar 5g

Ingredients:

- 85 of rice, uncooked

- 1/2 large head cabbage, thinly sliced

- ¼ tsp. of ground ginger

- 1/2 sliced onion

- 1/2 can (150 g) of tomatoes

- 1/2 apple, peeled and sliced

- 500 g of potatoes (2 or 3 medium), peeled and grated

- 1/2 tsp. of black pepper

- 1/2 tsp. of dried dill

- 1/2 egg white

Instructions:

- Spray the inside of the slow cooker using cooking spray. Then start layering the vegetables into the slow cooker. In a pressure cooker, combine one-third of the cabbage, one-third of the potatoes, one-third of the rice, one-third of the onion, one-third of the apple, and one-third of the seasonings and spices.

- Repeat twice more.

- Inside a mixing bowl, whisk the egg white till it becomes frothy. Mix in the tomatoes. Spoon this mixture on top of the vegetables.

- Cook on low for around 4 to 6 hours or till the vegetables are soft.

5. Spiced and Sweet Potatoes with Onions

Preparation time: 15 minutes | **Cooking time:** 7 to 8 hours | **Servings:** 2

Nutritional Value: Calories 172 | Total Fat 5g | Protein 3g | Carbs 30g | Sodium 275mg | Fiber 5g | Sugar 8g

Ingredients:

- 1/2 tsp. of ground cumin

- 2 large sweet potatoes, peeled and chopped

- 1/2 tbsp. of chili powder

- 20 ml of Vegetable Broth

- 1 jalapeño or habanero pepper, minced

- 1/2 onion, chopped

- 1 tbsp. of olive oil

- 2 minced garlic cloves

- 1/2 tsp. of salt

Instructions:

- Fill a 6-quart slow cooker halfway with all of the ingredients. Cook on low for around 7 to 8 hours or till the veggies are tender.

- Serve immediately after gently stirring the mixture.

Vegetarian Dishes

1. White Bean Casserole

Preparation time: 10 minutes | **Cooking time:** 8 hours | **Servings:** 2

Nutritional Value: Calories 256 | Total Fat 1g | Protein 17g | Carbs 49g | Sodium 286mg | Fiber 11g | Sugar 4g

Ingredients:

- 1/2 tbsp. of dried rosemary
- 250 g of dried white beans, soaked for overnight and rinsed
- 1/2 onion, finely chopped
- 400 ml of Vegetable Broth
- 1 tsp. of garlic powder
- 500 g of baby spinach
- Zest of 1/2 orange
- 1/4 tsp. of freshly ground black pepper
- 1/2 tsp. of sea salt

Instructions:

- Inside a slow cooker, combine the beans, salt, onion, rosemary, broth, garlic powder, orange zest, and pepper.
- Cook for around 8 hours on low flame, covered.
- Stir in the spinach for about 30 minutes before serving.

2. Sweet Honeyed Root Vegetables

Preparation time: 10 minutes | **Cooking time:** 6 to 8 hours | **Servings:** 2

Nutritional Value: Calories 102 | Total Fat 0g | Protein 2g | Carbs 49g | Sodium 177mg | Fiber 4g | Sugar 14g

Ingredients:

- 1 sweet potato, peeled and cut into chunks
- 1/2 medium-sized rutabaga, peeled and cut into chunks
- ½ tsp. of salt
- 2 large carrots, cut into chunks
- 1/2 onion, chopped
- 1 tbsp. of honey
- ⅛ tsp. of freshly ground black pepper

Instructions:

- Inside a 6-quart slow cooker, combine all of the ingredients and gently stir.

- Cook, covered, on low for around 6 to 8 hours or till the veggies are tender. Serve & enjoy.

3. Garlicky Lentils and Cauliflower with Rosemary

Preparation time: 10 minutes | **Cooking time:** 8 hours | **Servings:** 2

Nutritional Value: Calories 484 | Total Fat 2g | Protein 34g | Carbs 49g | Sodium 189mg | Fiber 32g | Sugar 2g

Ingredients:

- 1 tbsp. of fresh rosemary
- 1 tbsp. of extra-virgin olive oil
- 720 ml of low-sodium Vegetable Broth
- 250 g of cauliflower florets
- 1 tbsp. of roasted garlic
- Zest of 1 lemon
- 85 g of roughly chopped fresh parsley
- Freshly ground black pepper
- 250 g of lentils
- ⅛ tsp. of sea salt
- Juice of 1 lemon

Instructions:

- Add the cauliflower, olive oil, garlic, lentils, rosemary, and lemon zest to the slow cooker—season with black pepper and salt to taste.

- Pour the vegetable broth over the cauliflower and lentils. Cook for 8 hours on low flame, covered.

- Drizzle with lemon juice and sprinkle with parsley before serving.

4. Cheesy Broccoli and Rice Casserole

Preparation time: 10 minutes | **Cooking time:** 3 to 4 hours | **Servings:** 2

Nutritional Value: Calories 211 | Total Fat 14g | Protein 12g | Carbs 19g | Sodium 196mg | Fiber 4g | Sugar 2g

Ingredients:

- 100 ml jar of processed cheese spread
- 1/2 can (150 ml) of cream of mushroom soup
- 150 g pkg. of frozen chopped broccoli
- 170 g of rice, uncooked

Instructions:

- Mix the broccoli, rice, cheese spread, and soup inside the slow cooker.

- Cook for around 3 to 4 hours on high or till the broccoli and rice are tender but not soggy or dry.

5. Mushroom and Green Bean Casserole

Preparation time: 15 minutes | **Cooking time:** 6 hours | **Servings:** 2

Nutritional Value: Calories 274 | Total Fat 22g | Protein 9g | Carbs 10g | Sodium 298mg | Fiber 5g | Sugar 1g

Ingredients:

- 20 g of butter divided
- ½ chopped sweet onion
- 120 ml Chicken Broth
- 1/2 tsp. of minced garlic
- 20 g of grated Parmesan cheese
- 400 g of green beans, cut into 2-inch pieces
- 170 g of sliced button mushrooms
- 120 ml cream cheese

Instructions:

- Grease the inside of the slow cooker with 1 tablespoon of the butter.
- Inside a large-sized pan over medium-high flame, melt the rest of the butter. Stir in the onion, mushrooms, and garlic, and cook for 5 minutes, till the vegetables have softened.
- Add the green beans to the skillet, give them a good stir, and then move the whole thing to the insert.
- Put the cream cheese and broth inside a small-sized bowl and mix them with a whisk till they are smooth.
- Add the cheese mixture to the vegetables and stir it all together. Put the Parmesan cheese on top of the mixture.
- Cook on low for around 6 hours with the lid on.

- Serve immediately.

6. Mixed Bean Chili

Preparation time: 15 minutes | **Cooking time:** 6 to 8 hours | **Servings:** 2

Nutritional Value: Calories 257 | Total Fat 0g | Protein 13g | Carbs 58g | Sodium 1076mg | Fiber 17g | Sugar 1g

Ingredients:

- 250 g of frozen roasted corn kernels, thawed
- 1 tsp. of smoked paprika
- 1 can (450 g) of mixed beans, drained and rinsed
- 2 garlic cloves, minced
- 250 g of canned fire-roasted diced tomatoes, undrained
- 1 tsp. of dried oregano
- 170 g of diced onion
- 1 tsp. of ground cumin
- ⅛ tsp. of sea salt

Instructions:

- Put all of the ingredients into the slow cooker. Stir together quickly to mix.
- Cook on low for around 6 to 8 hours with the lid on.

7. Orange Yams with Apples

Preparation time: 15 minutes | **Cooking time:** 3 hours | **Servings:** 2

Nutritional Value: Calories 306 | Total Fat 5g | Protein 3g | Carbs 64g | Sodium 567mg | Fiber 4g | Sugar 2g

Ingredients:

- 1 tsp. of orange zest
- 1 apple, peeled, cored, thinly sliced
- 100 ml of orange juice
- 500 g of yams, drained
- A pinch of ground cinnamon
- 1 tbsp. of butter, melted
- 1/2 tsp. of salt
- 1 tbsp. of cornstarch
- 85 g of brown sugar

Instructions:

- Put the apples and yams inside the slow cooker.
- Orange zest and butter go in next.
- Mix the cornstarch, brown sugar, orange juice, salt, and cinnamon thoroughly in a bowl, then pour the mixture over the yams.
- Cover the cooker and cook on high for around 1 hour, then turn it to low and cook for 2 hours or till the apples are soft.

8. Zucchini Tomato Casserole

Preparation time: 15 minutes | **Cooking time:** 4 hours | **Servings:** 2

Nutritional Value: Calories 82 | Total Fat 5g | Protein 3g | Carbs 7g | Sodium 818mg | Fiber 2g | Sugar 4g

Ingredients:

- 1 tbsp. of extra-virgin olive oil
- 1 medium-sized zucchini, sliced
- 40 g of grated Parmesan cheese
- 1 medium red onion, sliced
- 1 green bell pepper, cut into thin strips
- ½ tsp. of basil
- 1/2 can (210 g) of diced tomatoes, with the juice
- 1 tsp. of sea salt
- ½ tsp. of black pepper

Instructions:

- Put the zucchini slices, onion slices, tomato slices, and bell pepper strips inside the slow cooker. Put basil, salt, and pepper on top.
- Cook on low for around 3 hours with the lid on.
- Pour the olive oil over the casserole and sprinkle the Parmesan on top. Cover the slow cooker and keep it on low for another hour and a half. Serve hot.

9. Red Bean, Carrot and Rice Gravy

Preparation time: 15 minutes | **Cooking time:** 6 hours | **Servings:** 2

Nutritional Value: Calories 237 | Total Fat 1g | Protein 15g | Carbs 47g | Sodium 421mg | Fiber 1g | Sugar 5g

Ingredients:

- 85 g of brown rice, uncooked

- 250 g of dried red beans

- 1/2 large onion, cut into chunks

- 2 carrots, peeled if you wish, and cut into chunks

- 400 ml of water

- 1/2 tbsp. of cumin

Instructions:

- Put the dried beans inside a slow cooker and cover them with water. Soak the beans for eight hours or all night. Drain the water and throw it away.

- Put the beans that have been soaked back in the slow cooker. Mix in the rest of the ingredients.

- Cover the slow cooker and cook on Low for around 6 hours or till all of the vegetables are soft.

10. Apple and Sweet Potatoes

Preparation time: 15 minutes | **Cooking time:** 6 hours | **Servings:** 2

Nutritional Value: Calories 312 | Total Fat 8g | Protein 3g | Carbs 39g | Sodium 289mg | Fiber 1g | Sugar 5g

Ingredients:

- 85 g of brown sugar

- 400g (about 6 medium) sweet potatoes or yams

- 160 ml of applesauce

- 2 tbsps. of butter, melted

- 1/4 tsp. of cinnamon

- Chopped nuts, optional

Instructions:

- If desired, peel the sweet potatoes. Cut it up into cubes or slices. Put everything in the slow cooker.

- Inside a mixing bowl, combine the butter, cinnamon, applesauce, and brown sugar. Drizzle over the potatoes.

- Cook on low flame for around 6 to 8 hours or till the potatoes are tender.

- If desired, mash the potatoes and sauce together using a large spoon, or spoon the potatoes into a serving dish and top with the sauce.

- If desired, top with nuts.

Poultry Dishes

1. Slow Cooker Spiced Chicken

Preparation time: 15 minutes | **Cooking time:** 7 to 9 hours | **Servings:** 2

Nutritional Value: Calories 184 | Total Fat 3g | Protein 30g | Carbs 11g | Sodium 316mg | Fiber 1g | Sugar 7g

Ingredients:

- 1 onion, chopped
- 4 (60 g each) boneless, skinless chicken thighs
- 1/2 tsp. of ground red chili
- 1 tbsp. of honey
- 1/2 tbsp. of chili powder
- 1 tbsp. of grated fresh ginger root
- 1/4 tsp. of ground cloves
- 2 minced garlic cloves
- ¼ tsp. of ground allspice
- 60 ml of freshly squeezed orange juice

Instructions:

- Use a knife to make diagonal lines on the chicken thighs so that the seasoning can penetrate deeper into the meat.
- Inside a small-sized mixing bowl, combine honey, ginger root, cloves, chili powder, chili powder, and five-spice powder. Spread this seasoning mixture evenly over the surface of the chicken and set aside.
- Inside the bottom of a 6-quart slow cooker, combine the onion and garlic. Serve the chicken over the veggies. Pour in the orange juice, cover, and cook for around 7 to 9 hours, or till the food thermometer reads 74°C. Serve right away!

2. Turkey Meatballs and Creamy Mushroom Gravy

Preparation time: 15 minutes | **Cooking time:** 3 to 8 hours | **Servings:** 2

Nutritional Value: Calories 638 | Total Fat 50g | Protein 24g | Carbs 5g | Sodium 412mg | Fiber 2g | Sugar 9g

Ingredients:

- 85 g of finely chopped celery
- 0.5 kg of ground turkey
- 1 egg, beaten

- 85 g of finely chopped onions

- 1 tbsp. of chopped fresh parsley

- 1 bay leave

- 1/4 tsp. of pepper

- 1/8 tsp. of garlic powder

- 1/2 tsp. of salt

- 140 ml of water

- 1/2 can (150 ml) cream of mushroom soup

- 85 g of bread crumbs

- 15 g pkg. of turkey gravy mix

- 1 tbsp. of cooking oil

- 1/2 tsp. of dried thyme

Instructions:

- Combine the turkey, bread crumbs, eggs, celery, garlic powder, onions, parsley, pepper, and salt inside a mixing bowl. Make 1 1/2-inch balls.

- Brown the meatballs in the oil in a skillet. Drain the meatballs and place them inside the slow cooker.

- Combine the soup, bay leaves, dry gravy mix, thyme, and water in a separate bowl. Pour the sauce over the meatballs.

- Cook on low for around 6 to 8 hours or on high for around 3 to 4 hours, covered. Before serving, remove the bay leaves.

- Over buttered noodles or mashed potatoes, serve.

3. Chicken Cassoulet

Preparation time: 15 minutes | **Cooking time:** 8 hours | **Servings:** 2

Nutritional Value: Calories 514 | Total Fat 1g | Protein 39g | Carbs 26g | Sodium 384mg | Fiber 8g | Sugar 4g

Ingredients:

- 1/2 tsp. of herbs de Provence

- Freshly ground black pepper

- 1/2 slice Applewood-smoked bacon, cut into strips

- 2 garlic cloves, smashed

- 1/2 small onion, halved and sliced thin

- 60 ml of low-sodium Chicken Broth

- 170 g of navy beans, drained and rinsed

- 1 bone-in, skinless chicken thigh (110 g) each

- ⅛ tsp. of sea salt

Instructions:

- Stir in the bacon, beans, herbes de Provence, garlic, onion, and broth till thoroughly combined. Arrange the chicken pieces on top of the beans— season with salt & a few grinds of black pepper.

- Cook for around 8 hours on low flame, covered.

4. Pesto-Glazed Chicken with Vegetables

Preparation time: 15 minutes | **Cooking time:** 6 to 8 hours | **Servings:** 2

Nutritional Value: Calories 533 | Total Fat 0g | Protein 33g | Carbs 33g | Sodium 740mg | Fiber 6g | Sugar 3g

Ingredients:

- ½ red onion halved and sliced thinly
- 150 g of grape tomatoes
- 1 tsp. of extra-virgin olive oil
- 1 zucchini, cut into 1-inch pieces
- 2 bone-in, skinless chicken thighs, about 230 g each
- 1 red bell pepper, cored and sliced thinly
- Freshly ground black pepper
- 1 tbsp. of assorted fresh herbs
- ⅛ tsp. sea salt
- 85 g of pesto

Instructions:

- Gently stir together the grape tomatoes, zucchini, onion, red bell pepper, and herbs inside the slow cooker. Pour in the olive oil. Season using salt and freshly ground black pepper to taste.
- Place the chicken inside a medium-sized bowl, coat it with pesto on all sides, and place it on top of the vegetables in the slow cooker.
- Cook on low for around 6 to 8 hours or till the chicken is cooked through and the veggies are tender.

5. Slow Cooked Turkey Loaf

Preparation time: 15 minutes | **Cooking time:** 6 to 7 hours | **Servings:** 2

Nutritional Value: Calories 120 | Total Fat 2g | Protein 23g | Carbs 3g | Sodium 55mg | Fiber 0g | Sugar 0g

Ingredients:

- 0.5 kg of fat-free ground turkey
- 1 tbsp. of poultry seasoning
- 1/2 egg
- 1 slice of bread, cubed

Instructions:

- Combine all of the ingredients inside a mixing bowl. Place the loaf inside the slow cooker in a round or oval shape.
- Cook on low for around 6 to 7 hours, covered. Remove the loaf from the slow cooker and set aside for 15 minutes before slicing & serving.

6. Balsamic Ginger Chicken

Preparation time: 15 minutes | **Cooking time:** 5 hours | **Servings:** 2

Nutritional Value: Calories 631 | Total Fat 28g | Protein 70g | Carbs 20g | Sodium 970mg | Fiber 1g | Sugar 5g

Ingredients:

- 2 bone-in chicken thighs (340 g), skin removed
- 1 tbsp. of cornstarch
- 1 medium carrot, sliced
- 1 tbsp. of brown sugar
- 2 chicken drumsticks (250 g), skin removed
- 1 tbsp. of balsamic vinegar
- 2 green onions, thinly sliced
- 3 garlic cloves, minced
- 1/4 tsp. of pepper
- 1 piece of fresh gingerroot (about 2 inches), peeled and thinly sliced
- 40 ml of soy sauce
- Hot cooked rice & minced fresh cilantro
- 1/2 tsp. of ground coriander
- 1 tbsp. of cold water

Instructions:

- Add the chicken, carrots, and green onions to a 3-quart slow cooker. Combine the garlic, coriander, ginger, soy sauce, brown sugar, vinegar, and pepper inside a small-sized bowl. Pour the mixture on top. Cover and cook on low for around 5-6 hours or till the chicken is tender.

- After cooking, transfer the chicken to a serving platter and keep it warm. Combine the juices inside a small-sized saucepan. Bring to boil. Stir together the water and cornstarch till smooth; gradually add to the pan. Bring to boil and cook, stirring constantly, for 1 to 2 minutes or till thickened. Garnish each serving with cilantro and serve with rice and chicken.

7. Garlicky Chicken Thigh with Mushroom

Preparation time: 15 minutes | **Cooking time:** 6 to 8 hours | **Servings:** 2

Nutritional Value: Calories 208 | Total Fat 2g | Protein 24g | Carbs 20g | Sodium 233mg | Fiber 1g | Sugar 4g

Ingredients:

- 2 bone-in, skinless chicken thighs, around 170 g each
- 1 tsp. of unsalted butter at room temperature or extra-virgin olive oil
- ⅛ tsp. of sea salt
- 1 minced shallot
- 2 minced garlic cloves

- 500 g of thinly sliced cremini mushrooms

- 1 tsp. of fresh thyme

- 3 tbsps. of dry sherry

- Freshly ground black pepper

Instructions:

- Grease the interior of the slow cooker with the butter.

- Toss the garlic, shallot, mushrooms, and thyme into the slow cooker to combine. Pour the sherry in.

- Season the chicken using pepper and salt and arrange the thighs on the mixture of mushrooms.

- Cook on low for around 6 to 8 hours, covered.

8. Onion Fennel Chicken with Sausage

Preparation time: 15 minutes | **Cooking time:** 8 hours | **Servings:** 2

Nutritional Value: Calories 341 | Total Fat 1g | Protein 24g | Carbs 7g | Sodium 292mg | Fiber 2g | Sugar 1g

Ingredients:

- 1 tsp. of extra-virgin olive oil

- ½ red onion halved and sliced thinly

- 2 bone-in, skinless chicken thighs, around 230 g each

- ½ fennel bulb, cored and sliced thinly

- 1 hot Italian sausage link, casing removed

- ⅛ tsp. of sea salt

Instructions:

- Add the onion, olive oil, and fennel to the slow cooker. To combine, gently stir everything together.

- Season the chicken using salt and place it on top of the onion & fennel.

- Crumble the sausage around the chicken.

- Cook for around 8 hours on low, covered.

9. Chicken Pot Pie

Preparation time: 15 minutes | **Cooking time:** 8 hours | **Servings:** 2

Nutritional Value: Calories 488 | Total Fat 6g | Protein 35g | Carbs 33g | Sodium 580mg | Fiber 8g | Sugar 1g

Ingredients:

- 250 g of diced onions

- 250 g of frozen peas, thawed

- 1 tbsp. of all-purpose flour

- 250 g of diced, peeled Yukon Gold potatoes

- 240 ml of low-sodium Chicken Broth

- 1 tsp. of fresh thyme

- 2 boneless and skinless chicken thighs, diced

- ⅛ tsp. of sea salt

- 250 g of diced carrots

- Freshly ground black pepper

Instructions:

- Add the peas, carrots, chicken, potatoes, onions, and thyme to the slow cooker. Season using salt and a few grinds of pepper. Toss the chicken and vegetables in the flour to coat. Add the chicken broth.

- Cook for around 8 hours on low, covered.

10. Chicken Roast with Potatoes

Preparation time: 15 minutes | **Cooking time:** 8 hours | **Servings:** 2

Nutritional Value: Calories 389 | Total Fat 6g | Protein 37g | Carbs 43g | Sodium 471mg | Fiber 3g | Sugar 1g

Ingredients:

- 90 ml of broth, tomato juice, or water

- 1/2 kg of skinless chicken breasts roast

- 1 large garlic clove, slivered

- 1/2 large onion, sliced

- 1 tbsp. of soy sauce

- 1/2 tbsp. of cornstarch

- 3 potatoes, cubed

- 1/2 tbsp. of cold water

Instructions:

- Make slits in the roast and stuff with garlic slivers. To brown, place under the broiler.

- Add half of the potatoes and onions to a slow cooker. On top of the onions and potatoes, place the browned roast. Cover with the rest of the onions.

- In a mixing bowl, combine the soy sauce and broth. Pour the sauce over the roast.

- Cook for around 8 hours on low, covered. Take the roast and veggies out of the liquid and slice the meat.

- Combine the cornstarch and water inside a mixing bowl. In the cooker, pour in the liquid. Increase to High and occasionally stir till thickened. Over the sliced vegetables and meat, serve.

Seafood Dishes

1. Fish Feast with Mixed Veggies

Preparation time: 15 minutes | **Cooking time:** 3 hours | **Servings:** 2

Nutritional Value: Calories 200 | Total Fat 2g | Protein 36g | Carbs 7g | Sodium 260mg | Fiber 2g | Sugar 3g

Ingredients:

- 0.5 kg of red snapper fillets
- 1/2 tbsp. of garlic, minced
- 20 ml of dry white wine or white grape juice
- 1/2 green bell pepper, cut into 1-inch pieces
- ¼ tsp. of salt
- 1/2 large onion, sliced
- 1 unpeeled zucchini, sliced
- 1/2 can (200 g) low-sodium diced tomatoes
- ¼ tsp. of black pepper
- ½ tsp. of dried oregano
- ½ tsp. of dried basil

Instructions:

- Spray the slow cooker using nonfat cooking spray.
- Rinse the snapper and pat it dry using a paper towel. Put everything in the slow cooker.
- Combine all of the remaining ingredients inside a large-sized mixing bowl and pour over the fish inside the slow cooker.
- Cook on high for around 2 to 3 hours, taking care not to overcook the fish.

2. Barbecue Tuna

Preparation time: 15 minutes | **Cooking time:** 4 to 10 hours | **Servings:** 2

Nutritional Value: Calories 138 | Total Fat 2g | Protein 18g | Carbs 14g | Sodium 311mg | Fiber 1g | Sugar 2g

Ingredients:

- 480 ml of tomato juice
- 2 tbsps. onion flakes
- 1 medium finely chopped green pepper
- 2 tbsps. of sugar
- 1 tbsp. of prepared mustard

- 2 tbsps. of Worcestershire sauce
- Dash of chili powder
- 1 can (340 g) of tuna, drained
- 3 tbsps. of vinegar
- Dash of hot sauce, optional
- 1 chopped rib of celery
- ½ tsp. of cinnamon

Instructions:

- Combine all of the ingredients inside the slow cooker.
- Cook on low for around 8 to 10 hours or on high for around 4 to 5 hours, covered. If the mixture becomes too dry while cooking, add 1/2 cup of tomato juice.
- Serve with buns after cooking.

3. Buttery Dijon-Lemon Fish

Preparation time: 15 minutes | **Cooking time:** 3 hours | **Servings:** 2

Nutritional Value: Calories 166 | Total Fat 9g | Protein 2g | Carbs 20g | Sodium 311mg | Fiber 1g | Sugar 2g

Ingredients:

- 2 tbsps. of Dijon mustard
- 680 g of orange roughy fillets
- 1 tsp. of Worcestershire sauce
- 42 g of butter, melted
- 1 tbsp. of lemon juice

Instructions:

- Fillets should be cut to fit inside the slow cooker.
- Pour the butter, lemon juice, Dijon mustard, and Worcestershire sauce over the fish. (If you must stack the fish, spoon some sauce over the first layer before adding the second layer.)
- Cook for around 3 hours on low or till the fish flakes easily but is not dry or overcooked.

4. Slow Cooker Shrimp with Grits

Preparation time: 15 minutes | **Cooking time:** 5 to 8 hours | **Servings:** 2

Nutritional Value: Calories 415 | Total Fat 10g | Protein 33g | Carbs 31g | Sodium 415mg | Fiber 5g | Sugar 5g

Ingredients:

- 0.5 kg of raw shrimp, peeled and deveined
- 250 of stone-ground grit
- 2 garlic cloves, minced
- 1 onion, chopped
- 1 green bell pepper, stemmed, seeded, and chopped
- 800 ml of Chicken Broth
- 1 bay leaf
- 150 g of shredded Cheddar cheese

- 1 large tomato, seeded and chopped
- 1 tsp. of Old Bay Seasoning

Instructions:

- Inside a 6-quart slow cooker, combine grits, bay leaves, onions, chicken broth, garlic, sweet peppers, tomatoes, and seasonings. Cook for around 5 to 7 hours on LOW, covered, till the coarse grains are tender and most of the liquid has been absorbed.
- Add the shrimp. Cook for around 30 to 40 minutes, or till the shrimp turns pink, with the lid on.
- Serve immediately after stirring in the cheese.

5. Savory Salmon with Barley

Preparation time: 15 minutes | **Cooking time:** 7 to 8 hours | **Servings:** 2

Nutritional Value: Calories 609 | Total Fat 20g | Protein 49g | Carbs 55g | Sodium 441mg | Fiber 13g | Sugar 4g

Ingredients:

- 1 red bell pepper, stemmed, seeded, and chopped
- 2 (140 g) of salmon fillets
- 1 fennel bulb, cored and chopped
- 40 g grated Parmesan cheese
- 250 g of hulled barley, rinsed
- 2 garlic cloves, minced

- 1/2 (110 g) package of cremini mushrooms, sliced
- 620 ml of Vegetable Broth
- 1 tsp. of dried tarragon leaves
- ⅛ tsp. of freshly ground black pepper

Instructions:

- Inside a 6-quart slow cooker, combine barley, tarragon, fennel, vegetable broth, garlic, bell peppers, mushrooms, and pepper. Cook for around 7 to 8 hours on low flame, till the barley, has soaked up most of the mixed soup and softened, and the veggies have also softened.
- Place the salmon fillets in the slow cooker. Cook, covered, for 20 to 40 minutes or until the salmon fillets test clean with a fork.
- Serve with a sprinkle of Parmesan cheese and salmon.

6. White Fish with Risotto

Preparation time: 15 minutes | **Cooking time:** 3 to 5 hours | **Servings:** 2

Nutritional Value: Calories 469 | Total Fat 12g | Protein 34g | Carbs 41g | Sodium 346mg | Fiber 5g | Sugar 2g

Ingredients:

- 250 g of short-grain brown rice
- 100 g of cremini mushrooms, sliced
- 250 g of baby spinach leaves

- 1/2 onion, chopped

- 600 ml of Vegetable Broth

- 2 garlic cloves, minced

- 1 tbsp. of unsalted butter

- 1/2 tsp. of dried thyme leaves

- 60 g grated Parmesan cheese

- 2 (140 g) of tilapia fillets

Instructions:

- Inside a 6-quart slow cooker, combine mushrooms, thyme, garlic, onions, rice, and vegetable broth. Cook for around 3 to 4 hours on low till the rice absorbs the sauce and softens.

- Place the fish on top of the rice. Cook, covered, for around 25 to 35 minutes or till the fillets are cooked through.

- Mix the fish into the risotto. Place baby spinach leaves on top.

- Mix in the butter and cheese. Simmer for 10 minutes on low heat. Serve right away!

7. Mixed Seafood Medley

Preparation time: 15 minutes | **Cooking time:** 3 to 4 hours | **Servings:** 2

Nutritional Value: Calories 346 | Total Fat 16g | Protein 14g | Carbs 45g | Sodium 412mg | Fiber 2g | Sugar 1g

Ingredients:

- 150 g of bay scallops

- 1 tbsp. of butter, melted

- 150 g of shrimp, peeled and deveined

- 1/2 (100 g) can of cream of celery soup

- 150 g of crab meat

- 1/2 tsp. of salt

- 1 tsp. of Old Bay seasoning

- 170 g soup can of milk

- 1/4 tsp. of pepper

Instructions:

- Layer the crab, shrimp, and scallops inside the slow cooker.

- Combine the milk with the soup inside a mixing bowl. Pour the sauce over the seafood.

- Add the salt, butter, pepper, and Old Bay seasoning to a separate bowl, mix well and pour over the top of the slow cooker.

- Cook on low for around 3 to 4 hours, covered.

- Serve over noodles or rice once cooked.

8. Salmon Dill and Potato Casserole

Preparation time: 10 minutes | **Cooking time:** 8 hours | **Servings:** 2

Nutritional Value: Calories 355 | Total Fat 5g | Protein 24g | Carbs 40g | Sodium 412mg | Fiber 5g | Sugar 1g

Ingredients:

- 240 ml of 2% milk

- Freshly ground black pepper

- 1 tsp. of butter at room temperature

- 100 g of smoked salmon

- 2 eggs

- ⅛ tsp. of sea salt

- 2 medium russet potatoes, peeled and sliced thinly

- 1 tsp. of dried dill

Instructions:

- Lightly coat the inside of the slow cooker with butter.

- Inside a small-sized bowl, whisk together the milk, salt, eggs, dill, and a few grinds of black pepper.

- Spread one-third of the potatoes in a single layer on the bottom of the slow cooker and top with one-third of the salmon. Pour one-third of the egg mixture over the salmon. Layer the remaining salmon, potatoes, and egg mixture on top.

- Cook, covered, on low for around 8 hours.

9. Boiled Fish with Carrots

Preparation time: 10 minutes | **Cooking time:** 7 to 9 hours | **Servings:** 2

Nutritional Value: Calories 263 | Total Fat 9g | Protein 28g | Carbs 19g | Sodium 357mg | Fiber 5g | Sugar 9g

Ingredients:

- 1 purple carrot, peeled and sliced

- 1/2 tsp. of dried marjoram leaves

- 1 large orange carrot, peeled and sliced

- 2 (140 g) of trout fillets

- 1 bay leaf

- 2 garlic cloves, minced

- 1 yellow carrot, peeled and sliced

- ½ tsp. of salt

- 1 onion, chopped

- 60 ml of Vegetable Broth

Instructions:

- Inside a 6-quart slow cooker, combine carrots, bay leaf, onions, garlic, marjoram, vegetable broth, and salt. Cook for around 7 to 9 hours on low, covered, till the carrots are tender.

- Remove the bay leaves and set them aside. Inside a slow cooker, place the trout fillets. Cook for another 20 to 30 minutes or till the fillet can be peeled off with a fork.

10. Lemony Fish

Preparation time: 10 minutes | **Cooking time:** 3 to 4 hours | **Servings:** 2

Nutritional Value: Calories 160 | Total Fat 5g | Protein 22g | Carbs 7g | Sodium 870mg | Fiber 2g | Sugar 3g

Ingredients:

- 1 lemon divided

- 300 g of frozen firm-textured fish fillets, thawed

- 1 bay leaf

- 2 whole peppercorns

- 1 onion, thinly sliced

- 2 tbsps. of butter, melted

- 140 ml of water

- 1 tsp. of salt

Instructions:

- Cut the fillets into serving-size pieces.

- Combine 1 sliced lemon, salt, onion slices, bay leaf, butter, and peppercorns inside a mixing bowl and pour into the slow cooker.

- Arrange the fillets on top of the lemon and onion slices. Pour in some water.

- Cook for around 3 to 4 hours on high with the lid on.

- Before serving, carefully remove the fish fillets with a slotted spoon. Place on a heat-resistant plate.

- Sprinkle with half of the second lemon juice. Garnish with the remaining lemon slices if desired.

Meat Dishes

1. Salisbury Steak with Mushroom Sauce

Preparation time: 20 minutes | **Cooking time:** 6 hours | **Servings:** 2

Nutritional Value: Calories 500 | Total Fat 39g | Protein 33g | Carbs 5g | Sodium 550mg | Fiber 2g | Sugar 3g

Ingredients:

- 85 g of almond flour

- 2 tbsps. of extra-virgin olive oil, divided

- 250 g of sliced mushrooms

- 25 ml of heavy (whipping) cream

- 1/2 egg

- 1 scallion, white and green parts, chopped

- 300 g of ground beef

- 1 tsp. of minced garlic

- ½ chopped sweet onion

- 1/2 tbsp. of Dijon mustard

- 2 tbsps. of chopped fresh parsley for the garnish

- 150 ml of Beef Broth

- Freshly ground black pepper

- 90 ml heavy (whipping) cream

- Salt

Instructions:

- Grease the inside of the slow cooker with 1 tablespoon of the olive oil.

- Mix the beef, scallion, almond flour, heavy cream, egg, and garlic together inside a medium-sized bowl. Make four patties that are about 1 inch thick.

- Inside a large-sized skillet, heat the last 2 tablespoons of olive oil over medium-high flame. Add the patties, sear them on both sides for about 5 minutes, then move them to the insert.

- Put the onion & mushrooms inside the pan and cook them for three minutes.

- Put the mustard and broth inside the skillet, and move the sauce to the insert.

- Cook on low for around 6 hours with the lid on.

- Take the patties out and put them on a plate. Add the cream to the sauce and whisk it well.

- Add pepper and salt to the sauce.

- Put the sauce on top of the patties, sprinkle with the parsley, and serve.

2. Lamb Chops with Potatoes

Preparation time: 10 minutes | **Cooking time:** 8 hours | **Servings:** 2

Nutritional Value: Calories 419 | Total Fat 4g | Protein 27g | Carbs 43g | Sodium 326mg | Fiber 6g | Sugar 2g

Ingredients:

- 60 ml of red wine

- 1 tsp. of extra-virgin olive oil

- 1/2 tsp. of smoked paprika

- 85 g of diced roasted red pepper

- 1 red potato, unpeeled, & quartered

- 1 tbsp. of fresh parsley

- 1 bone-in trimmed of fat lamb shoulders

- 1/2 tsp. of minced garlic

- 1/4 tsp. of sea salt

- Freshly ground black pepper

- 85 g of diced onion

- 1/4 tsp. of minced fresh rosemary

Instructions:

- Grease the inside of the slow cooker using the olive oil.

- Add the wine, parsley, red pepper, onion, and parsley, and stir.

- Inside a small-sized bowl, mix together the garlic, paprika, salt, rosemary, and a few turns of the black pepper mill. Use this mixture to rub on the lamb chops. Or, you can do this a day ahead of time to let the rub's flavors soak into the meat. Place the chops on top of the onion & wine mix inside the slow cooker. To fit, the chops might have to touch a little bit.

- Put the potatoes on top of the lamb.

- Cook on low for around 8 hours with the lid on.

3. Shepherd's Pie

Preparation time: 20 minutes | **Cooking time:** 8 hours | **Servings:** 2

Nutritional Value: Calories 468 | Total Fat 6g | Protein 45g | Carbs 42g | Sodium 203mg | Fiber 8g | Sugar 2g

Ingredients:

- 330 g of prepared mashed potatoes

- 250 g of frozen peas, thawed

- 1/8 tsp. of sea salt

- 250 g of diced carrots

- Freshly ground black pepper

- 230 g of lean ground beef

- 170 g of diced onions

- 2 tbsps. of shredded sharp Cheddar cheese

Instructions:

- Put the peas, carrots, onions, and beef inside the slow cooker and mix everything together well. Season the mix with salt and black pepper.

- Spread the mashed potatoes out evenly over the meat and vegetable mixture.

- Cook on low for around 8 hours with the lid on.

- Sprinkle the Cheddar cheese on top of the shepherd's pie and serve.

4. Slow Cooked Creamy Pork Chops

Preparation time: 10 minutes | **Cooking time:** 4 to 5 hours | **Servings:** 2

Nutritional Value: Calories 656 | Total Fat 26g | Protein 18g | Carbs 39g | Sodium 432mg | Fiber 4g | Sugar 1g

Ingredients:

- 2 tbsps. of ketchup

- 1 chopped onion

- 1 tsp. of Worcestershire sauce

- 2 whole pork chops, boneless or bone-in, divided

- 1/2 can (150 g) of 98% fat-free cream of chicken soup

Instructions:

- Mix the chopped onions & soup together inside a bowl. Mix well after adding the Worcestershire sauce and ketchup. Half of the mixture should be put in the slow cooker.

- Throw the pork chops in the slow cooker. If you need to stack them, spoon a portion of the remaining sauce over the first layer of chops.

- Then add the next layer of chops. Pour the rest of the sauce on top to cover.

- Cover the slow cooker and cook on low for around 4 to 5 hours or till the meat becomes tender but not dry.

5. Slow-Cooked Lamb Shanks with Veggies

Preparation time: 10 minutes | **Cooking time:** 4 to 10 hours | **Servings:** 2

Nutritional Value: Calories 67 | Total Fat 3g | Protein 7g | Carbs 3g | Sodium 187mg | Fiber 4g | Sugar 1g

Ingredients:

- 1 medium thinly sliced onion

- ¼ tsp. pepper

- 1 small carrot, cut into thin strips

- 1 tsp. dried oregano

- 1 rib celery, chopped

- 1–2 cloves of garlic, split

- 60 ml of dry white wine

- 1 tsp. salt

- 1/2 can (110 g) tomato sauce

- 1 tsp. dried thyme

- 1 bay leave, crumbled

- 1 1/2 lamb shanks, cracked

Instructions:

- Put the onions, carrots, and celery inside the slow cooker.

- Salt and pepper the lamb after rubbing it with garlic. Put the food inside the slow cooker.

- Mix the rest of the ingredients inside a separate bowl, then add them to the vegetables and meat.

- Cook on Low for around 8 to 10 hours or on High for around 4 to 6 hours with the lid on the slow cooker.

6. Slow Cooker Balsamic Glazed Roast Beef

Preparation time: 15 minutes | **Cooking time:** 7 to 8 hours | **Servings:** 2

Nutritional Value: Calories 476 | Total Fat 39g | Protein 28g | Carbs 2g | Sodium 214mg | Fiber 0g | Sugar 1g

Ingredients:

- 1/2 tbsp. of minced garlic

- 2 tbsps. of extra-virgin olive oil, divided

- 400 g of boneless beef chuck roast

- 120 ml of Beef Broth

- 1/2 tbsp. of granulated erythritol

- 1/4 tbsp. of chopped fresh thyme

- 60 ml of balsamic vinegar

- ½ tsp. of red pepper flakes

Instructions:

- Lightly grease the slow cooker's insert with 1 tablespoon of the olive oil.

- Inside a large-sized skillet, heat the last 2 tablespoons of olive oil over medium-high flame. Put the beef in the pan and brown it on all sides, which should take about 7 minutes. Move to the insert.

- Put the rest of the ingredients into a small bowl and whisk them until they are all mixed together.

- Pour the sauce over the beef.

- Cook on low for around 7 to 8 hours with the lid on.

- Turn off when you're done cooking, and serve warm.

7. Pork Tenderloin in Cranberry-Mustard Sauce

Preparation time: 10 minutes | **Cooking time:** 6 to 8 hours | **Servings:** 2

Nutritional Value: Calories 354 | Total Fat 6g | Protein 40g | Carbs 34g | Sodium 342mg | Fiber 3g | Sugar 9g

Ingredients:

- 2 tbsps. of brown sugar

- 1 pork tenderloin, about 400 g total

- 2 tbsps. of Dijon mustard

- 1 tbsp. of lemon juice

- 1/2 can (240 ml) of whole cranberry sauce

Instructions:

- Inside a small-sized bowl, mix together the mustard, brown sugar, cranberry sauce, and lemon juice. About a third of the mixture should go in the slow cooker's bottom.

- Add the tenderloins on top of the sauce. Pour the rest of the sauce over the meat.

- Cover the slow cooker and cook on low for around 6 to 8 hours or till the meat is tender.

- Wait 10 minutes before you slice the meat.

8. Beef Broccoli

Preparation time: 15 minutes | **Cooking time:** 6 hours | **Servings:** 2

Nutritional Value: Calories 471 | Total Fat 6g | Protein 52g | Carbs 29g | Sodium 907mg | Fiber 3g | Sugar 2g

Ingredients:

- 2 tbsps. of low-sodium soy sauce

- 340 g of flank steak, sliced thinly

- 1 tsp. of toasted sesame oil

- 480 ml of broccoli florets

- 2 tbsps. of honey or maple syrup

- 1 tsp. of minced garlic

- 120 ml of low-sodium Beef Broth

- 1 tbsp. of cornstarch

Instructions:

- Put the flank steak and broccoli inside the slow cooker.

- Inside a measuring cup or small-sized bowl, whisk together the sesame oil, honey, soy sauce, beef broth, garlic, and cornstarch. Pour this mix on top of the beef and broccoli.

- Cook on low for around 6 hours with the lid on.

9. Pork Chops with Baked Beans

Preparation time: 10 minutes | **Cooking time:** 4 to 6 hours | **Servings:** 2

Nutritional Value: Calories 467 | Total Fat 12g | Protein 34g | Carbs 67g | Sodium 319mg | Fiber 4g | Sugar 6g

Ingredients:

- 2 rib pork chops, ½-inch thick

- 1 tbsp. of brown sugar

- 1 (240 g) can of baked beans

- 1 tsp. of prepared mustard

- 3 onion slices, ¼-inch thick

- 1 tbsp. of ketchup

Instructions:

- Put the baked beans inside the bottom of a slow cooker that has been greased.

- On top of the beans, put the pork chops.

- Spread mustard on top of the chops. Then sprinkle brown sugar on top and drizzle ketchup over it.

- Put the slices of onion on top.

- Cook on High for around 4 to 6 hours with the lid on.

10. Spiced Leg of Lamb

Preparation time: 10 minutes | **Cooking time:** 8 hours | **Servings:** 2

Nutritional Value: Calories 218 | Total Fat 8g | Protein 32g | Carbs 4g | Sodium 202mg | Fiber 0g | Sugar 1g

Ingredients:

- 1/4 tsp. of ground cinnamon

- 1/2 tsp. of garlic powder

- 1/4 tsp. of sea salt

- 1 tsp. of onion powder

- 1/4 tsp. of dried marjoram

- 1/2 (400 g) of boneless leg of lamb, butterflied

- 1 tsp. of dried oregano

- 1/2 tsp. of dried thyme

- 1/4 tsp. of ground nutmeg

- 120 ml of Beef Broth

- 1/4 tsp. of freshly ground black pepper

Instructions:

- Inside a small-sized bowl, mix the onion powder, salt, garlic powder, marjoram, nutmeg, cinnamon, thyme, oregano, and pepper. Cover the lamb with the mixture.

- Pour the broth over the lamb inside the slow cooker.

- Cook on low for around 8 hours with the lid on. Serve the lamb cut into pieces.

Soups and Stews

1. Vegetable and Chicken Stew

Preparation time: 20 minutes | **Cooking time:** 6 hours | **Servings:** 2

Nutritional Value: Calories 276 | Total Fat 22g | Protein 17g | Carbs 6g | Sodium 271mg | Fiber 2g | Sugar 4g

Ingredients:

- 200 ml of Chicken Broth
- 2 tbsps. of extra-virgin olive oil, divided
- 1/2 chopped sweet onion
- 1 diced celery stalk
- 1/2 diced carrot
- 1 tsp. of minced garlic
- 220 g of chicken thighs, diced into 1½-inch pieces
- 1/2 tsp. of dried thyme
- 170 g of shredded kale
- Salt
- 100 ml of coconut cream
- Freshly ground black pepper

Instructions:

- Grease the inside of the slow cooker with 1 tablespoon of the olive oil.
- Inside a large-sized skillet, heat the last 2 tablespoons of olive oil over medium-high heat. Stir in the chicken and cook it for about 7 minutes or till it is almost done.
- Add the garlic and onion, stir, and cook for 3 more minutes.
- Place the chicken mixture inside the slow cooker and stir in the celery, carrot, broth, and thyme.
- Cook on low for around 6 hours with the lid on.
- Mix well after adding the coconut cream and kale.
- Salt and pepper it, and serve it hot.

2. Fennel, Potato and Leek Soup

Preparation time: 20 minutes | **Cooking time:** 8 hours | **Servings:** 2

Nutritional Value: Calories 200 | Total Fat 4g | Protein 7g | Carbs 32g | Sodium 269mg | Fiber 7g | Sugar 2g

Ingredients:

- 1 peeled and diced white potato

- 480 ml of low-sodium Chicken Broth

- 1 cored and chopped fennel bulb

- 1 tsp. of ground fennel seed

- 2 tbsps. of heavy cream

- 1 leek, white and pale green parts only, sliced thinly

- 1 sprig of fresh tarragon, roughly chopped

- ⅛ tsp. of sea salt

- 1 tsp. of white wine vinegar or lemon juice

Instructions:

- Put the fennel bulb, salt, fennel seed, leek, potato, and broth inside the slow cooker and stir to mix. Cook on low for around 8 hours with the lid on.

- Stir the vinegar into the slow cooker, and then use an immersion blender to puree the soup. Mix well after adding the heavy cream.

- If you want, sprinkle fresh tarragon on top and serve.

3. Hearty Pumpkin and Turkey Stew

Preparation time: 20 minutes | **Cooking time:** 7 to 8 hours | **Servings:** 2

Nutritional Value: Calories 356 | Total Fat 27g | Protein 21g | Carbs 11g | Sodium 312mg | Fiber 4g | Sugar 1g

Ingredients:

- 2 tbsps. of extra-virgin olive oil, divided

- 220 g of boneless turkey breast, cut into 1-inch pieces

- 1/2 leek, thoroughly cleaned and sliced

- 140 ml of coconut milk

- 1 tsp. of minced garlic

- 240 ml of Chicken Broth

- 1 celery stalk, chopped

- 1/2 carrot, diced

- 1 tsp. of chopped thyme

- 250 g of diced pumpkin

- Salt

- 1/2 scallion, white and green parts, chopped, for garnish

- Freshly ground black pepper

Instructions:

- Grease the inside of the slow cooker with 1 tablespoon of the olive oil.

- Inside a large skillet, heat the last 2 tablespoons of olive oil over medium-high flame. Add the turkey, stir, and cook for 5 minutes, till the meat is browned.

- Add the garlic and leek, stir, and cook for 3 more minutes.

- Place the turkey mixture in the slow cooker and mix in the coconut milk, broth, carrot, pumpkin, celery, and thyme.

- Cook on low for around 7 to 8 hours with the lid on.

- Add pepper and salt to taste.

- Add the scallion, and it's ready to eat.

4. Slow Cooker Split Pea Soup

Preparation time: 10 minutes | **Cooking time:** 4 to 8 hours | **Servings:** 2

Nutritional Value: Calories 51 | Total Fat 0g | Protein 1g | Carbs 12g | Sodium 448mg | Fiber 2g | Sugar 0g

Ingredients:

- 170 g of green or yellow split peas, rinsed well

- 1/2 tbsp. of dried thyme

- 400 ml of water

- 1 tsp. of salt, plus additional as needed

- 1 small sweet potato, cut into ½-inch dice

Instructions:

- Inside a slow cooker, mix together the water, split peas, thyme, sweet potatoes, and salt.

- Cover the slow cooker and cook on low for around 8 hours or on high for 4 hours.

- Using an immersion blender or a regular blender, blend half or all of the soup till

smooth, being careful with the hot liquid. You may need to do this in batches.

- Taste the soup and add more salt or pepper if it needs it.

5. Garlicky Carrot Chicken Soup with Kale

Preparation time: 10 minutes | **Cooking time:** 6 hours | **Servings:** 2

Nutritional Value: Calories 361 | Total Fat 3g | Protein 45g | Carbs 20g | Sodium 354mg | Fiber 3g | Sugar 0g

Ingredients:

- 2 boneless and skinless chicken thighs, diced

- ⅛ tsp. of red pepper flakes

- 6 garlic cloves, roughly chopped

- 2 carrots, peeled and diced

- 1 small onion, halved and sliced thin

- Zest of 1 lemon

- 480 ml of low-sodium Chicken Broth (page 216)

- ⅛ tsp. of sea salt

- 500 g of shredded fresh kale

- Juice of 1 lemon

Instructions:

- Put everything except the lemon juice and kale inside the slow cooker and stir to mix.

- Cook on low for around 6 hours with the lid on.

- Mix well after adding the lemon juice and kale.

6. Spiced Garlic Beef Stew with Pearl Barley

Preparation time: 10 minutes | **Cooking time:** 8 hours | **Servings:** 2

Nutritional Value: Calories 536 | Total Fat 4g | Protein 55g | Carbs 20g | Sodium 262mg | Fiber 6g | Sugar 1g

Ingredients:

- ½ tsp. of ground coriander

- 60 ml of red wine vinegar

- 85 g of dry pearl barley

- 170 g of minced onions

- 120 ml of water

- Freshly ground black pepper

- ½ tsp. of ground cinnamon

- 2 minced garlic cloves

- 1 tbsp. of tomato paste

- ⅛ tsp. of sea salt

- 240 ml of dry red wine

- 2 tbsps. of minced fresh flat-leaf parsley

- 340 g of beef brisket, cut into 1-inch cubes

- 85 g of minced celery

Instructions:

- Put the pearl barley and water inside the slow cooker and stir till all of the barley is submerged.

- Inside a large-sized bowl, mix the coriander, vinegar, cinnamon, black pepper, salt, tomato paste, and red wine. Stir the beef, celery, onions, garlic, and parsley together in the bowl. Pour this mixture very slowly over the barley. No stirring.

- Cook on low for around 8 hours with the lid on.

7. Creamy Garlic Poblano and Corn Chowder

Preparation time: 10 minutes | **Cooking time:** 8 hours | **Servings:** 2

Nutritional Value: Calories 519 | Total Fat 6g | Protein 16g | Carbs 40g | Sodium 158mg | Fiber 10g | Sugar 6g

Ingredients:

- 120 ml of heavy cream or half-and-half

- 2 poblano chilies, fire-roasted, peeled and seeded

- 240 ml of Chicken Stock

- 2 garlic cloves, minced

- 1 medium onion, chopped

- 1 can (210 g) of cream-style corn

- 1/4 tsp. of ground cumin

- 1 medium russet potato, peeled and diced

- 2 tbsps. of chopped fresh cilantro

- 250 g of fresh or frozen corn

Instructions:

- Put everything into the slow cooker except for the cilantro and cream.

- Cover the slow cooker and cook on low for around 8 hours or on high for around 4 hours.

- Mix well after adding the cream. Taste the food and add or take away spices as needed. Add the chopped cilantro, and it's ready to serve.

8. Herbed Garlic Mushroom Soup

Preparation time: 10 minutes | **Cooking time:** 8 hours | **Servings:** 2

Nutritional Value: Calories 158 | Total Fat 4g | Protein 7g | Carbs 14g | Sodium 203mg | Fiber 2g | Sugar 1g

Ingredients:

- 1 onion, halved, cut into thin half circles

- 230 g of cremini mushrooms, washed and quartered

- 1 tsp. of fresh thyme

- 30 g of dried wild mushrooms

- ½ tsp. of minced fresh rosemary

- 480 ml of low-sodium Chicken Broth

- ⅛ tsp. of sea salt

- 2 tbsps. of dry sherry

- 60 ml of heavy cream

- 2 garlic cloves, minced

Instructions:

- All of the ingredients, except for the heavy cream, should be put inside the slow cooker and stirred together.

- Cook on low for 8 hours with the lid on.

- Just before you serve, add the heavy cream and mix it well.

9. Bacon Cauliflower and Chicken Soup

Preparation time: 15 minutes | **Cooking time:** 6 hours | **Servings:** 2

Nutritional Value: Calories 540 | Total Fat 44g | Protein 35g | Carbs 6g | Sodium 203mg | Fiber 1g | Sugar 0g

Ingredients:

- 170 g of chopped cooked bacon

- 1 tbsp. of extra-virgin olive oil

- 240 g of shredded cheddar Cheese

- 240 ml of coconut milk

- 500 ml of Chicken Broth

- 60 ml of cream cheese, cubed

- 1/2 sweet onion, chopped

- 250 g of chopped cauliflower

- 250 g of chopped cooked chicken

- 1 tsp. of minced garlic

Instructions:

- Grease the inside of the slow cooker with a little olive oil.

- Put the chicken, cauliflower, coconut milk, broth, onion, bacon, and garlic in the cooker.

- Cook on low for around 6 hours with the lid on.

- Mix well after adding the cream cheese and cheese, and then serve.

10. Apple, Butternut Squash and Parsnip Soup

Preparation time: 15 minutes | **Cooking time:** 8 hours | **Servings:** 2

Nutritional Value: Calories 179 | Total Fat 2g | Protein 3g | Carbs 38g | Sodium 192mg | Fiber 5g | Sugar 1g

Ingredients:

- 170 g of peeled, diced parsnip

- 1 Granny Smith apple, cored, peeled, and diced

- 1 sprig of fresh thyme

- 85 g of diced onion

- 250 g of peeled, diced butternut squash

- 230 ml of low-sodium Vegetable Broth

- 1 tbsp. of heavy cream

- 1/4 tsp. of sea salt

Instructions:

- All of the ingredients, except for the heavy cream, should be put inside the slow cooker and stirred together.

- Cook on low for around 8 hours with the lid on. Take out the thyme sprig and stir in the heavy cream.

- Use an immersion blender to make the soup smooth.

Desserts

1. Blueberry Pecan Crisp

Preparation time: 15 minutes | **Cooking time:** 3 to 4 hours | **Servings:** 2

Nutritional Value: Calories 222 | Total Fat 19g | Protein 9g | Carbs 9g | Sodium 11mg | Fiber 4g | Sugar 21g

Ingredients:

- 500 g of blueberries
- 170 g of ground pecans
- 1/2 egg
- 2 tbsps. of coconut oil, melted, divided
- 1/2 tsp. of baking soda
- 1/4 tsp. of ground cinnamon
- 1 tbsp. of coconut milk
- 85 g plus 2 tbsps. of granulated erythritol

Instructions:

- Lightly grease a 4-quart slow cooker using 1 tablespoon of the coconut oil.
- Add the blueberries and 2 tablespoons of erythritol to the slow cooker's insert.
- Add the last 3/4 cup of erythritol, the baking soda, the ground pecans, and the cinnamon to a large-sized bowl and stir till everything is well mixed.
- Stir in the egg, coconut milk, and the rest of the coconut oil. Stir till the mixture looks like coarse crumbs.
- Put the pecan mixture in the insert, then put the egg mixture on top of that.
- Cover the slow cooker and cook on low for around 3 to 4 hours.
- Serve warm, and enjoy.

2. Vanilla Lemon Custard Dessert

Preparation time: 15 minutes | **Cooking time:** 3 hours | **Servings:** 2

Nutritional Value: Calories 319 | Total Fat 30g | Protein 7g | Carbs 3g | Sodium 15mg | Fiber 0g | Sugar 28g

Ingredients:

- 1/2 tsp. of pure vanilla extract
- 30 ml freshly squeezed lemon juice
- ⅓ tsp. of liquid stevia
- 240 ml of heavy (whipping) cream

- 2 egg yolks

- 120 ml of whipped coconut cream

Instructions:

- Inside a medium-sized bowl, whisk together the liquid stevia, lemon juice and zest, yolks, and vanilla.

- Mix the heavy cream in well with a whisk, then divide the mixture between four 113-gram ramekins.

- Put a rack at the bottom of the slow cooker's insert and set the ramekins on it.

- Pour enough water so that it comes halfway up the sides of the ramekins.

- Cover and cook for around 3 hours on low.

- Take the ramekins out of the insert and let them cool till they are at room temperature.

- Put the ramekins in the fridge to chill for a long time. Serve with whipped coconut cream on top.

3. Baked Apples with Brown Sugar

Preparation time: 15 minutes | **Cooking time:** 2 to 5 hours | **Servings:** 2

Nutritional Value: Calories 319 | Total Fat 30g | Protein 2g | Carbs 47g | Sodium 11mg | Fiber 4g | Sugar 34g

Ingredients:

- 1 tbsp. of chopped walnuts

- 1/4 tsp. of ground cinnamon

- 4 medium baking apples, cored but left whole and unpeeled

- 60 ml of water

- 85 g of brown sugar

- Frozen yogurt

Instructions:

- Put chopped walnuts and sugar inside a small-sized bowl. Blend well.

- Put the apples inside the slow cooker's bottom. Put the mixture in the middle of the apple with a spoon and divide it evenly between the apples.

- On top of the apple filling, sprinkle cinnamon.

- Put a half cup of water around the edge of the slow cooker.

- Cook on low for around 3 to 5 hours with the lid on.

- Serve with frozen yogurt.

4. Sweet Peach Brown Betty

Preparation time: 20 minutes | **Cooking time:** 5 to 6 hours | **Servings:** 2

Nutritional Value: Calories 322 | Total Fat 9g | Protein 6g | Carbs 57g | Sodium 69mg | Fiber 6g | Sugar 31g

Ingredients:

- 1 tbsp. of freshly squeezed lemon juice

- 85 g of coconut sugar

- 4 ripe peaches, peeled and cut into chunks

- 170 g of dried cranberries

- 250 g of cubed whole-wheat bread

- 2 tbsps. of Honey

- 1/4 tsp. of ground cardamom

- 40 ml of melted coconut oil

- 170 g of whole-wheat bread crumbs

Instructions:

- Inside a 6-quart slow cooker, mix the peaches, lemon juice, dried cranberries, and honey.

- Inside a large-sized bowl, mix the bread cubes, coconut sugar, bread crumbs, and cardamom. Spread the coconut oil that has been melted over everything and mix it well.

- The bread mixture is sprinkled on top of the fruit inside the slow cooker.

- Close the lid and cook on low for around 5 to 6 hours, till the fruit is bubbling and the top has turned brown. Serve warm!

5. Apple Caramel with Vanilla Dessert

Preparation time: 15 minutes | **Cooking time:** 6 hours | **Servings:** 2

Nutritional Value: Calories 775 | Total Fat 58g | Protein 72g | Carbs 57g | Sodium 17mg | Fiber 4g | Sugar 26g

Ingredients:

- 1 medium apple, peeled, cored, and cut into wedges

- 60 ml of apple juice

- 1/2 tsp. of vanilla

- 2 to 4 slices of angel food cake

- 1/8 tsp. of ground cardamom

- 100 g of caramel candy

- 1/4 tsp. of ground cinnamon

- 30 ml of creamy peanut butter

- Vanilla ice cream

Instructions:

- Inside a slow cooker, put apple juice, vanilla, caramel candies, and spices.

- Put 1 teaspoon of peanut butter and apple wedges inside the slow cooker. Stir well.

- Cover and cook for around 5 hours on low.

- Stir well, and keep cooking on Low for another hour.

- On each piece of angel cake, put 1/3 cup of the hot mixture and a scoop of ice cream.

6. Honey Yogurt with Mangoes

Preparation time: 10 minutes | **Cooking time:** 10 hours | **Servings:** 2

Nutritional Value: Calories 206 | Total Fat 3g | Protein 9g | Carbs 31g | Sodium 128mg | Fiber 2g | Sugar 19g

Ingredients:

- 60 ml of plain yogurt

- 2 mangoes, cut into chunks

- 1000 ml of 2% milk

- ¼ tsp. of ground cardamom

- 1 tbsp. of honey

Instructions:

- Pour the milk into the slow cooker. Cover and cook for around 2 hours on low.

- Disconnect the slow cooker and stir well after adding the yogurt. Use the lid to cover the slow cooker, and use a bath towel to wrap the outside of the pot to help it stay warm. Give it 8 hours or the whole night to rest.

- Arrange a few layers of cheesecloth over a medium bowl, pour the mixture in, and let it drain for 10 to 15 minutes for thick

yogurt. The whey left in the cheesecloth can be thrown away or saved to make smoothies.

- Mix well after adding the mango chunks, honey, and cardamom. Refrigerate leftovers.

7. Slow Cooker Savory Berry Crisp

Preparation time: 10 minutes | **Cooking time:** 5 to 6 hours | **Servings:** 2

Nutritional Value: Calories 219 | Total Fat 8g | Protein 5g | Carbs 37g | Sodium 9mg | Fiber 7g | Sugar 12g

Ingredients:

- 170 g of frozen organic blueberries

- 1/2 tsp. of ground cinnamon

- 170 g of frozen organic strawberries

- 40 ml of coconut oil, melted

- 170 g of frozen organic raspberries

- 170 g of whole-wheat flour

- 250 g of rolled oats

- 85 g of maple sugar

- 1/2 tbsp. of lemon juice

Instructions:

- Put frozen berries inside a slow cooker with a 6-quart capacity without letting them thaw first. Pour lemon juice on top.

- Inside a large-sized bowl, mix the oats, maple syrup, flour, and cinnamon together. Add the melted coconut oil and stir till the mixture becomes crumbly.

- Pour the mixture of oatmeal and milk over the fruit inside the slow cooker.

- Cook on Low with the lid on for about 5 to 6 hours, till the fruit is bubbling and the top is brown. Serve right away!

8. Spiced Berry and Pumpkin Compote

Preparation time: 10 minutes | **Cooking time:** 3 to 4 hours | **Servings:** 2

Nutritional Value: Calories 113 | Total Fat 9g | Protein 4g | Carbs 7g | Sodium 5mg | Fiber 3g | Sugar 19g

Ingredients:

- 170 g of cranberries

- 1/2 tbsp. of coconut oil

- 1/4 tsp. of ground allspice

- 60 ml of coconut milk

- 250 g of diced pumpkin

- 170 g of blueberries

- A pinch of tsp. ground nutmeg

- 1/2 tsp. of ground cinnamon

- Juice and zest of 1 orange

- 85 g of granulated erythritol

- 120 ml of whipped cream

Instructions:

- Lightly grease the inside of the slow cooker with the coconut oil.

- Put everything but the whipped cream in the slow cooker, except for the whipped cream.

- Cover the slow cooker and cook on low for around 3 to 4 hours.

- After cooking, let the compote cool for an hour, then put a big scoop of whipped cream on top and serve it warm.

9. Vanilla Spiced Pear Butter

Preparation time: 15 minutes | **Cooking time:** 6 to 8 hours | **Servings:** 2

Nutritional Value: Calories 230 | Total Fat 1g | Protein 1g | Carbs 60g | Sodium 0mg | Fiber 12g | Sugar 45g

Ingredients:

- 1.4 kg of unpeeled pears, cored and cut into chunks

- 1 tbsp. of freshly squeezed lemon juice

- ½ tsp. of ground ginger

- 2 tsps. of ground cinnamon

- 120 ml of water

- 1 tsp. of vanilla extract

- 1 ½ tsps. of coconut sugar (optional)

Instructions:

- Mix together the lemon juice, ginger, pears, vanilla, cinnamon, and water inside the slow cooker.

- Cover the pot and cook it on low for around 6 to 8 hours. When the food is done cooking, put it in a blender or food processor and blend it till it is smooth.

- Taste it and add more coconut sugar if you think it needs it. Put inside a container that won't let air in and store in the fridge.

10. Cinnamon Gingerbread

Preparation time: 10 minutes | **Cooking time:** 3 hours | **Servings:** 2

Nutritional Value: Calories 259 | Total Fat 23g | Protein 7g | Carbs 6g | Sodium 0mg | Fiber 3g | Sugar 15g

Ingredients:

- 1 tbsp. of coconut flour

- 1/4 tsp. of ground nutmeg

- 1/8 tsp. of ground cloves

- 1 tbsp. of coconut oil

- 85 g of granulated erythritol

- 1 tsp. of baking powder

- 2 eggs

- 1 tbsp. of ground ginger

- 1/2 tsp. of pure vanilla extract

- 1 tsp. of ground cinnamon

- Pinch of salt

- 60 ml of butter, melted

- 250 g of almond flour

- 90 ml of heavy (whipping) cream

Instructions:

- Lightly grease the inside of the slow cooker with coconut oil.

- Mix the erythritol, cloves, almond flour, coconut flour, cinnamon, baking powder, nutmeg, ginger, and salt together in a large bowl.

- Inside a medium-sized bowl, whisk together the butter, vanilla, heavy cream, eggs, and vanilla extract.

- Put the wet ingredients together with the dry ones.

- Put the batter in the insert with a spoon.

- Cover the slow cooker and cook on low for around 3 hours or till a toothpick stuck in the middle comes out clean.

- Serve warm, and enjoy.

Shopping List

A

Almond milk

Aged ham

Almond flour

Apple

Apple juice

Almonds

All-purpose flour

Avocado

Applesauce

Acorn squash

B

Bell peppers

Black pepper

Blueberries

Butter

Breakfast sausage

Baking powder

Bacon

Basil leaves

Baby peas

Black beans

Beef broth

Brown beech mushrooms

Barley

Bay leaves

Butternut squash

Baking soda

Beef brisket

Baked beans

Boneless beef chuck roast

Bay scallops

Bread

Balsamic vinegar

Brown rice

Broccoli

Baby spinach

Beef skirt steak

Brown sugar

C

Coconut oil

Cheddar Cheese

Coconut milk

Canned pumpkin purée

Cranberries

Cream cheese

Condensed Cheddar cheese soup

Cottage cheese

Chicken broth

Chili powder

Cilantro

Cheese tortellini

Chicken breasts

Condensed cream chicken soup

Carrots

Condensed cream of mushroom soup

Coconut flour

Crab meat

Caramel candy

Cardamom

Chickpeas

Chicken bouillon cubes

Cabbage

Cauliflower

Cumin

Corn kernels

Cheese Whiz

Coconut sugar

Cornstarch

Cinnamon

Chopped nuts

Celery

D

Dried cherries

Dried apricots

Dried cranberries

Dried chipotle

Dry Italian-style salad dressing mix

Dijon mustard

Dry sherry

Dry white wine

Dried red beans

Dried black mushrooms

Dried dill

E

Egg

Elbow macaroni

Evaporated milk

Egg noodles

F

Flank steak

Fresh herbs

Fennel bulb

Frozen peas

Flour

G

Ginger

Garlic

Ground cinnamon

Granulated erythritol

Ground cloves

Ground nutmeg

Ground pecans

Ground allspice

Garlic salt

Ground cardamom

Ground ginger

Ground beef

Ground red chili

Ground turkey

Green beans

Grape tomatoes

Green onions

Ground mixed peppercorns

Gold potatoes

Garlic powder

H

Honey

Hard cheese

Heavy cream

Heavy whipping cream

Hot sauce

Herbs de Provence

I

Italian sausage

Italian seasoning

J

Jalapeño

K

Kale

Kalamata olives

L

Lean ground beef

Lasagna noodles

Leek

Lamb shanks

Lentils

Lemon juice

M

Maple extract

Mashed potato flakes

Milk

Mozzarella cheese

Marinara sauce

Maple sugar

Mustard

Mangoes

Mashed potatoes

Marjoram leaves

N

Navy beans

O

Olive oil

Oregano

Orange juice

Orange zest

Orange roughy fillets

Old Bay Seasoning

Orange

Oyster mushrooms

P

Pecans

Protein powder

Peaches

Pumpkin

Parsley

Pears

Paprika

Parmesan cheese

Pesto

Peanut butter

Poblano chilies

Parsnip

Pork chops

Pork tenderloin

Purple carrot

Pimientos

Pumpkin pie spice

Poultry seasoning

Parsnip

Q

Quinoa

R

Rolled oats

Red bell pepper

Red snapper fillets

Raspberries

Rib pork chops

Red wine

Red potatoes

Rutabaga

Romaine

Rosemary

S

Salt

Scallion

Sweet onion

Steel-cut oats

Strawberries

Split peas

Steak seasoning

Sweet peppers

Salsa

Sesame oil

Salmon fillets

Sweet potato

Soy sauce

Shiitake mushrooms

Shrimp

Stone-ground grit

T

Tomato sauce

Trout fillets

Tomato paste

Tomato

Tarragon leaves

Tilapia fillets

Tuna

Taco seasoning mix

Turkey gravy mix

Thyme

U

Unsweetened almond milk

Unsweetened apple juice

V

Vanilla extract

Vegetable Stock

Vinegar

W

Whole-grain bread

Whole milk

Whole-wheat flour

White wine vinegar

Whole cranberry sauce

Worcestershire sauce

White grape juice

White mushrooms

White rice

Wild rice

Wheat berries

White beans

Y

Yogurt

Z

Zucchini

28-Days Meal Plan

Days	Breakfast	Snack	Lunch	Snack	Dinner
1	Slow Cooker Spiced Pear Oatmeal	Baked Apples with Brown Sugar	Beef Broccoli	Blueberry Pecan Crisp	Chicken Cassoulet
2	Slow Cooker Vanilla Pumpkin and Pecan Oatmeal	Cheese and Mushrooms Meatballs	Fish Feast with Mixed Veggies	Slow Cooker Steak Salad with Lime Cilantro Dressing	Mushroom and Green Bean Casserole
3	Cheesy Ham Casserole	Cheese Stuffed Jalapeño Peppers	Slow Cooker Rice with Chicken	Vanilla Lemon Custard Dessert	Hearty Pumpkin and Turkey Stew
4	Vanilla Cinnamon Pumpkin Pudding	Cheesy Tortellini	Salisbury Steak with Mushroom Sauce	Sweet Peach Brown Betty	Spiced Garlic Beef Stew with Pearl Barley
5	Oatmeal with Berry	Cinnamon Gingerbread	Red Bean, Carrot and Rice Gravy	Slow Cooker Mac and Cheese	Shepherd's Pie
6	Creamy Mashed Potatoes	Slow Cooker Spiced Applesauce	Pork Chops with Baked Beans	Honey Cranberry Stuffed Acorn Squash	Creamy Garlic Poblano and Corn Chowder
7	Garlicky Bacon Egg Casserole	Apple Crumble with Peach	Vegetable and Chicken Stew	Cheese and Mushrooms Meatballs	Fish Feast with Mixed Veggies

8	Quinoa Hot Cereal with Cranberry	Vanilla Lemon Custard Dessert	Lamb Chops with Potatoes	Cheese Stuffed Jalapeño Peppers	Apple, Butternut Squash and Parsnip Soup
9	Layered Vegetable Cheese and Egg Casserole	Quinoa Salad with Feta and Arugula	Mixed Bean Chili	Honey Yogurt with Mangoes	Slow Cooked Creamy Pork Chops
10	Vanilla Quinoa and Fruit Breakfast	Honey Cranberry Stuffed Acorn Squash	Turkey Meatballs and Creamy Mushroom Gravy	Cheesy Tortellini	Herbed Garlic Mushroom Soup

11	Peppers Stuffed with Sausage, Egg and Cheese	Blueberry Pecan Crisp	Fennel, Potato and Leek Soup	Baked Apples with Brown Sugar	Savory Salmon with Barley
12	Quinoa Hot Cereal with Cranberry	Rosemary Garlic New Potatoes	Mushroom and Green Bean Casserole	Slow Cooker Spiced Apple sauce	Slow-Cooked Lamb Shanks with Veggies
13	Slow Cooker Spiced Pear Oatmeal	Sweet Peach Brown Betty	Zucchini Tomato Casserole	Apple Caramel with Vanilla Dessert	Slow Cooker Split Pea Soup

14	Vanilla Cinnamon Pumpkin Pudding	Slow Cooker Steak Salad with Lime Cilantro Dressing	Pesto-Glazed Chicken with Vegetables	Honey Cranberry Stuffed Acorn Squash	Bacon Cauliflower and Chicken Soup
15	Creamy Mashed Potatoes	Slow Cooker Savory Berry Crisp	Creamy Garlic Poblano and Corn Chowder	Apple Crumble with Peach	Chicken Cassoulet
16	Garlicky Bacon Egg Casserole	Apple Caramel with Vanilla Dessert	Slow Cooker Balsamic Glazed Roast Beef	Rosemary Garlic New Potatoes	Red Bean, Carrot and Rice Gravy

17	Vanilla Quinoa and Fruit Breakfast	Honey Yogurt with Mangoes	Garlicky Carrot Chicken Soup with Kale	Cinnamon Gingerbread	Beef Broccoli
18	Layered Vegetable Cheese and Egg Casserole	Baked Apples with Brown Sugar	Shepherd's Pie	Rosemary Garlic New Potatoes	Slow Cooker Rice with Chicken
19	Cheesy Ham Casserole	Slow Cooker Savory Berry Crisp	Savory Salmon with Barley	Sweet Peach Brown Betty	Mixed Bean Chili

20	Peppers Stuffed with Sausage, Egg and Cheese	Apple Crumble with Peach	Slow Cooked Creamy Pork Chops	Quinoa Salad with Feta and Arugula	Lamb Chops with Potatoes
21	Slow Cooker Vanilla Pumpkin and Pecan Oatmeal	Cheese and Mushrooms Meatballs	Slow-Cooked Lamb Shanks with Veggies	Honey Yogurt with Mangoes	Pork Chops with Baked Beans
22	Vanilla Cinnamon Pumpkin Pudding	Vanilla Lemon Custard Dessert	Fish Feast with Mixed Veggies	Blueberry Pecan Crisp	Turkey Meatballs and Creamy Mushroom Gravy

23	Slow Cooker Spiced Pear Oatmeal	Honey Cranberry Stuffed Acorn Squash	Hearty Pumpkin and Turkey Stew	Cheese and Mushrooms Meatballs	Fennel, Potato and Leek Soup
24	Vanilla Quinoa and Fruit Breakfast	Quinoa Salad with Feta and Arugula	Bacon Cauliflower and Chicken Soup	Apple Caramel with Vanilla Dessert	White Fish with Risotto
25	Oatmeal with Berry	Rosemary Garlic New Potatoes	Slow Cooker Balsamic Glazed Roast Beef	Apple Crumble with Peach	Zucchini Tomato Casserole

26	Creamy Mashed Potatoes	Sweet Peach Brown Betty	Mixed Bean Chili	Slow Cooker Steak Salad with Lime Cilantro Dressing	Salisbury Steak with Mushroom Sauce
27	Garlicky Bacon Egg Casserole	Slow Cooker Spiced Applesauce	Lamb Chops with Potatoes	Honey Cranberry Stuffed Acorn Squash	Mushroom and Green Bean Casserole
28	Quinoa Hot Cereal with Cranberry	Apple Caramel with Vanilla Dessert	Chicken Cassoulet	Baked Apples with Brown Sugar	Pesto-Glazed Chicken with Vegetables

Measurement Conversion Chart

CUP	OUNCES	MILLILITERS	TABLESPOONS
8 cup	64 oz.	1895 ml	128
6 cup	48 oz.	1420 ml	96
5 cup	40 oz.	1180 ml	80
4 cup	32 oz.	960 ml	64
2 cup	16 oz.	480 ml	32
1 cup	8 oz.	240 ml	16
3/4 cup	6 oz.	177 ml	12
2/3 cup	5 oz.	158 ml	11
1/2 cup	4 oz.	118 ml	8
3/8 cup	3 oz.	90 ml	6
1/3 cup	2.5 oz.	79 ml	5.5
1/4 cup	2 oz.	59 ml	4
1/8 cup	1 oz.	30 ml	3
1/16 cup	1/2 oz.	15 ml	1

Conclusion

We hope you've been inspired to use that slow cooker that's been collecting dust in your closet after reading this book. Slow cooker is an indispensable kitchen appliance. They can be used to make everything from main courses to appetizers and desserts. They are extremely adaptable. We hope that after reading this book, you will be inspired to use that crock pot that has been collecting dust in your closet. Crock pots are a must-have kitchen appliance. You can use them to make everything from main courses to appetizers and desserts. They are very adaptable. It is difficult to burn anything in them, and the recipes almost always turn out well. The best part is that there is almost never any fuss. Simply pour the ingredients in and let them sit for a while. You can even cook in a slow cooker while at work and eat it when you get home.

Use your slow cooker for family meals or parties. For a potluck supper, you can even serve your food directly from the slow cooker placed on the table. Slow cooking has the advantage of retaining flavor and moisture in a recipe much better than baking, which creates liquids and flavors to evaporate.

A slow cooker is essential, especially if you are short on time. Simply combine all of the ingredients and cook your dinner during the night or while you are at work, and you will wake up or come back home to a delicious meal. Isn't that incredible?

This cookbook contains the most delectable British meals from breakfast to dinner. Hopefully, the pages of this book will assist you in creating one of the most delicious recipes with simple instructions for yourself, your family, and your friends. Good luck!

Recipe Index

Printed in Great Britain
by Amazon

20461694R00052